COMMUNICATION EFFICIENCY AND RURAL DEVELOPMENT IN AFRICA

The Case of Cameroon

EMMANUEL K. NGWAINMBI, PH.D.

UNIVERSITY
PRESS OF
AMERICA

Lanham • New York • London

Copyright © 1995 by
University Press of America,® Inc.
4720 Boston Way
Lanham, Maryland 20706

3 Henrietta Street
London WC2E 8LU England

Library of Congress Cataloging-in-Publication Data

Ngwainmbi, Komben Emmanuel.
Communication efficiency and rural development in Africa : the case
of Cameroon / Emmanuel K. Ngwainmbi.
p.   cm.
Includes bibliographical references.
1. Communication in rural development—Cameroon.   I. Title.
HN819.Z9C6   1994   307.1'412—dc20   94–33063 CIP

ISBN 0–8191–9734–3 (cloth : alk. paper)
ISBN 0–8191–9735–1 (pbk. : alk. paper)]

Contents

CHAPTER FIVE
METHODS OF RESEARCHING
DEVELOPMENT INFORMATION

CHAPTER SIX
DATA ANALYSIS AND FINDINGS ON
RADIO AND TV PROGRAMS

CHAPTER SEVEN
FINDING A NEW COMMUNICATION
AGENDA FOR RURAL DEVELOPMENT

Tables

Figures

Abbreviations

ABC   American Broadcasting Corporation
BBC   British Broadcasting Corporation
CAMCULD   Cameroon Credit Union League. This is an affiliate to
                    the Confederation of African Savings and Credit
                    Cooperatives whose headquarter is in Nairobi, Kenya.
CBS   Central Broadcasting Service
CFA   *Communauté Financière Africaine.* Members of this
                    currency include: Benin, Burkina Faso, Cameroon,
                    Central African Republic, Chad, Comoros Island, Congo,
                    Equatorial Guinea, Gabon, Ivory Coast, Mali (which had
                    its own currency before joining in 1981), Niger, Senegal,
                    and Togo.
CIDA   Canadian International Development Agency
CPDM   Cameroon People's Democratic Movement (the ruling
                    party of Cameroon)
CNN   Cable News Network
CRTV   Cameroon Radio and Television
FAO   Food and Agriculture Organization
FONADER   (french) An organization that provides funds to help
                    farmers improve their work in Cameroon.
FRCN   Federal Radio Corporation of Nigeria
IMF   International Monetary Fund
MIDENO   An outreach community development agency in the
                    Northwest Province of Cameroon heavily funded by
                    foreign agencies. As a people-oriented entity, it oversees
                    agricultural, handicraft, and other development-related
                    activities in the rural areas. However, like other
                    associations, it offers limited material assistance to the
                    needy. Its personnel has been reduced.
MINFOC   Ministry of Information and Culture (Cameroon)
NBC   National Broadcasting Corporation (U.S.A.)
NTA   Nigerian Television Authority
NWCA   Northwest Cooperative Association (Cameroon). Its
                    administration is located in various urban and rural areas
                    in the province.

NWICO	New World Information and Communication Order
NATO	North Atlantic Treaty Organization
NRRC	National Rural Radio Competition
OCORA/ OCORP	*Office de Coopération Radio Phonique*
PMO	Produce Marketing Organization (Cameroon)
PTV	Pedagogic Television
SDF	Social Democratic Front. A political party formed in 1992
UCAO	(french) Union of Cocoa farmers headquartered in the Southwest Province (Cameroon). Like NWCA and MIDENO, it engages in the production and marketing of cash crops.
UDEAC	*Union Douanière et économique de l'Afrique Centrale*
UNDP	United Nations Development Project
UNESCO	United Nations Educational, Scientific, and Cultural Organization
UNICEF	United Nations International Children's Emergency Fund
USIA	United States Information Agency
WADA	Wum Area Development Authority. Located in the Northwest Province of Cameroon. Funded primarily by the German government, it employed skilled and unskilled people from around the country. It also helped to improve the production skills of farmers and craftspeople and promoted self-reliant activities and such social activities as soccer. It managed a second division soccer club, but the organization is defunct.

CHAPTER 1

COMMUNICATION AND DEVELOPMENT POLICY

While participating at the recent World Economic Development Congress held in Washington, D.C.'s Shoreham hotel, I was impressed by the amount of interest in Africa shown by world investors. Many papers dwelled on investment opportunities there. The presenters looked at Africa as the next economic superpower. There has been too much talk about bad leadership and increasingly weak economies in Africa, but little has been said about how to resolve these problems.

This book fills that gap. It provides new information on those issues and proposes several means of expediting development, including collective participation between policymakers and the rural citizens, since the latter constitute over 80% of Africa's 600,000,000 people. With the global community coming together under one political and economic umbrella, it is important for the "dark" continent to create and use information for the development of the masses, the rural areas.

African policymakers delay development because they undervalue the rural areas and concentrate on redeveloping the urban areas which their neocolonial trust powers visit. Preferring urban redeveloping to rural change leads to rural exodus. This book seeks:

1. To add to existing communication literature, especially for students researching development communication, an increasingly useful field
2. To inform scholars and organizations interested in international affairs, politics, and development, and potential foreign businesswomen /men interested in doing business in rural areas in Africa

3. To inform telecommunication industries and development technicians that have targeted or may be targeting rural areas
4. To inform development agencies like the World Bank, United Nations Development Project, UNESCO, and IMF, and,
5. To direct foreign governments interested in designing and executing development programs in Cameroon and other African countries

When many African countries received independence from European administrators in the 1960s, Africans trained by Europeans became preoccupied with constructing a nationalist culture among their citizens. In Somalia, it was Mohammed Said Barre, in Zaire Mobutu, in Gabon Omar Bongo, in Ethiopia Haile Selaisse, in Uganda Idi Amin, in the Ivory Coast Houphouet Boigney, in Kenya Jomo Kenyatta, in Cameroon Ahmadou Ahidjo.

Even heads of state of the Second Republics and other influential policymakers stressed the need for their citizens to cultivate a patriotic and progressive spirit. For noted Pan-Africanist Kwame Nkrumah, a progressive African front required a strong feeling of nationhood, of belonging.

This novel hysteria for national and continental unity can be best achieved through the use of the mass media. Faringer (1991) pointed out that the fundamental objective of the African mass media after independence was to promote this unity (p. 76). In the 1960s, President Kenyatta went forward by identifying the newspaper as a viable tool for communicating understanding among the nationals, so long as it reported with accuracy.

Kenyatta said:

> The press in Africa can have a tremendous influence in nation building
> . . . . It may constantly inspire the spirit of Harambee or National
> Unity which every young country needs as the fundament of its
> progress (Kenyatta, 1968, p. 3).

He suggested that African governments raise money and provide equipment and personnel for the newspapers in their countries. That message also echoed in Somalia and Cameroon, as their governments charged the press with the role of promoting nationalist ideologies. A Somali official is said to have stated in a communique:

It is the function of the nation's communication media to weld the entire community into a single entity, a people of the same mind and possessed of the same determination to safeguard the national interest (Lamb, 1986, p. 245).

Cameroon's President, Paul Biya, in his text *Communal Liberalism* (1987) asked Cameroonians to demonstrate a strong civic and national spirit. Biya also asked the mass media to promote national development and defend the interest of Cameroon internationally.

The struggle for national development in Africa has focused on such positive aspects as integrating and democratizing and such negative connotations as brainwashing Africans about the nature of national unity. Since the eastern and western regions reunited in 1972, the Cameroon government has been asking its citizens to cultivate a sense of unity and progress. Such a goal would require designing and disseminating entertainment and development messages to the rural people who constitute about 75% of the country's population, instead of government propaganda. In private newspapers, especially *Le Messager, Our People, Cameroon Post,* and *The Herald,* the government has been heavily criticized for promoting an agenda that suits the objectives of the ruling party, CPDM, through the Cameroon electronic media. The question, then, is whether the Cameroon mass media satisfy the information needs of the rural people whose low social and economic standards deserve public attention. It can be argued that citizens who have little access to useful information about their country are denied the right to participate in the development of their nation. Such is the predicament in which some African rural people may find themselves.

What can rural residents in Africa do to bring Africa to the Second World level? A point where Africans will be economically independent? What can be done to destigmatize Africa as Third World?

In the wake of rapid ideological and infrastructural change all over the world today, many rural people do not get adequate information from the mass media and, therefore, cannot take advantage of available technology to change their environment. Individual problems that could be solved or prevented through shared information remain undetected and unresolved.

What does it take to detect problems? Some development theorists argue that disseminating ideas to change basic political and social beliefs is crucial to the citizens of developing countries. According to Dahrendorf (1959) and Verba (1965), policymakers are reluctant to change the political culture of their own societies because they do not want to change their own beliefs, values and interests. Another theorist asserts that residents of developing countries have been ignored by the system when they compare their present and anticipated achievements with their past experiences (Langer, 1979).

Langer explains that citizens resent their government for not addressing their immediate problems. This statement implies that governments and citizens do not have a strong intermediary to collect, process and disseminate information concerning living conditions. There should be more effective interaction between the two entities, to bring about a higher standard of living. Participatory democracy can only be effective through communication.

It is in this light that President Biya demanded that the media and Cameroonians find ways to increase their material and mental well-being (Biya, 1987, pp. 85-87). He meant that they should reduce the practices that encourage poor health, improper role modeling, and destitution and encourage cultural, spiritual and religious aspirations (1987, p. 89). This concept of development requires a steady flow of rural development information between the Cameroon government and the Cameroon rural public.

In rural communities in Africa, people appear less eager to carry out self-reliant development projects because of rampant belief in and practice of witchcraft and superstition, inadequate foreign support, and harsh climatic conditions. In some rural communities where the land is mostly mountainous, many people are not zealous about operating village projects. Many of these people become sick and die because of minimal and restricted health care and nutritional information. Between 1990 and 1994, when the civil servants in Cameroon were not receiving their salaries regularly, some rural residents who had been depending on their government-employed relatives for economic relief died of malnutrition and disease. A university professor on a campaign trail in remote villages reported an average of 16 mostly young people dying daily per village. Yet the Cameroon government is not making the best use of the mass media to provide significant and relevant information to help curb these problems among the rural population.

Since over 75% of Cameroon's population is rural, national development will be difficult to attain if the interests of the rural people are not served. Development planners must consider the opinions of village people, and necessary messages should be communicated to and from government policymakers through both broadcast and traditional communications media.

The Media Spark Physical Improvement

Although the mass media's role in Third World development activities has been both overlooked and overstressed, mass media have been useful in assessing the social, political and cultural development of developing countries. International communication scholars recommend that governments of developing countries create and broadcast programs nationwide to advance their educational, political and cultural development (Tsurutani, 1973). The reason people in remote African communities are helpless to solve development problems is that there is not adequate development information for the benefit of rural people in the public media. The problems of development include inefficient agricultural techniques, poor nutrition, poor family planning, population growth, low life expectancy, poor health care, bad or temporary roads, and resource shortages. The poor condition of the roads, for example, isolates villages, thereby slowing the communication of information, village activities, and development projects that require collective participation.

Africa's development problems can be reduced through the extensive development of programs in radio, television, music, shows, and theaters. Historical research shows that mass media have been used successfully to support development in African and other Third World countries. Social, political, and economic development strategies disseminated via the broadcast and traditional mass media are encouraged by most African governments *(Revue de L'Urtna,* 1981). The use of mass media campaigns to revolutionize developing areas was encouraged by Ainslie (1966). In *The Press in Africa: Communication, Past and Present* the scholar posits that efficient development can be planned only through the use of sufficient mass communication.

The mass media are a public institution. Edeani (1990) concurs. The newspaper, Edeani states, is devoted to protecting and serving public interest. Momeka (1980) adds that courageous reporting and editing increase newspaper readership and sales. Case studies of the media's social responsibility have been documented in Tanzania, Nigeria, Ethiopia, and Senegal, to name a few.

Tanzania

Radio broadcasts have been helpful in supporting political participation, national independence, health care, food production, nutrition, and related constructs of progressive change. The Tanzanian experience started in 1967 when nongovernmental organizations used radio campaigns to influence public opinion. Instructional radio has been used there to elicit feedback and to direct organized learning groups. In 1969, messages on socialism were broadcast on radio in Tanzania. Dodds (1972) and Grenholm (1975) reported that radio was able to teach civic obligations and practical skills to the rural residents. The strategy for this responsibility, Momeka (1994) argues, requires cooperation and guided listening. It also requires learning techniques, support materials, instructors, and some assessment of the results (p. 129).

Nigeria

Mass media have proven very useful in changing peoples' attitudes in Nigeria. Nigeria's health care policymakers adopted a mass media campaign to promote immunization among mothers in rural areas. In 1989, the United Nations mobilized local administrative agents, professional and civic groups, and the mass media to support the immunization of children against pertussis, tetanus, diphtheria and related diseases. In order to increase the number of children vaccinated, Nigerian health care policymakers staged a multimedia campaign using television, radio, mobile vans with loudspeakers, posters, action groups, and religious leaders. According to Ogundimu (1994), the mobilization campaign was so successful that UNICEF the Federal Radio Corporation of Nigeria (FRCN), and the Nigerian Television Authority (NTA) reached an agreement wherein UNICEF would provide broadcasting equipment, transportation and funding to the latter agencies in return for the production and dissemination of messages for child survival.

Ethiopia

The support of the mass media in development efforts in Eritrea and Ethiopia improved political relations between the countries. In a 1993 study funded by the World Bank, indigenous media — songs, theatre, and churches — were used to spread information on the incorporation of women's rights into the political development of those countries.

Senegal

The Senegalese development experience started in 1969 when radio provided rural education through community group listening and feedback (Berrigan, 1981, p. 22). But the debut was not without problems. Rural residents, for whom the program was meant, were embarrassed that their private values were being contaminated and their personal secrets were being exposed to the public. They might have been mesmerized by the magic of the radio — this small thing with a large voice and an ability to tell people what to do. Community participation became intense only through a campaign by Senegalese government over *radio educative rurale*. Berrigan (1981) states that listeners increased dramatically. Today, several development programs are broadcast on Senegalese radio. A more detailed examination of the results of instructional media appears in Chapter Four.

Mass communication seems, indeed, to be instrumental in influencing change in developing countries. Extensive developmental programs in radio, TV and traditional communication could reduce development setbacks in Africa. Cultivation theorists contend that mass media should, as their main function, dispense a common image and influence the behavior of a diverse population in a heterogeneous culture. According to Littlejohn (1983), people's reactions to messages they see and/or hear through the media depend considerably on the way the messages are sent and interpreted. The mood of the message receiver can also affect his or her actions at the time he or she receives the message. Thus messages broadcast on audio-visual media should be stated in simple and comprehensive language, and their dissemination schedules should give all audience members equal access to them. The timing of programs broadcast and the exact meaning of the message must be seriously considered by the message sender.

Broadcast messages interpreted for the common person by civil servants and/or the literate elite are often inflated with innuendos. This kind of two-step information flow diminishes the credibility and alters the original meaning of messages, which are then interpreted by the average listener in a very different manner than had been intended.

The manner in which messages in African media are interpreted depends also on where the original information stemmed from and in what language it was broadcast. Messages on government or national issues are disseminated mainly in French and English and are, thus, often assimilated only by the literate few because most rural residents do not speak these languages. People developing media programs have no input from the rural residents who make up 75% of the country's population.

Information ministers charge that the Cameroon mass media should serve the country and contribute to its development policies. One of these policies dwells on balanced development as advocated in the nationally broadcast speeches of President Biya and the Secretary General of Cameroon's main opposition party, the Social Democratic Front. Balanced development demands that the Cameroon government establish its social and infrastructure projects equally throughout Cameroon.

Since the government asked those who could control the Cameroon mass media to support development in Cameroon, did the government pay any attention to rural development media programs? Did the government carefully assess the activities of the media? Did the Cameroon government encourage more media programs on rural health care awareness, agriculture, rural cooperative activities, rural nutrition, or other activities in the village to support interethnic relations? These questions will be answered in Chapter Six.

African Authorities Support Communication Input

Pan-Africanist Kwame Nkrumah (1964) and President Julius Nyerere of Tanzania have all called on developing countries to have organized patterns of information to build their society. Since information is knowledge, information for development purposes will depend on the internal organization of each country. Given the potential usefulness of the broadcast and popular traditional media for disseminating development messages, more concepts, strategies and plans are necessary to expedite the use of the media to disseminate development information to the people of Cameroon.

The Cameroon government has stated a policy that requires the media to contribute substantially to national and public education. The government's words do not always reflect its actions. Cohen (1963) has also observed that the media do not tell people what to think, but are successful in telling them what to think about (p. 13). Thinking involves constructing images in the mind, or what Lipmann (1946) first referred to as "pictures in our heads" (p. 11). Since the mass media tend to influence people to think about phenomena in a certain way, issues not only become public agendas but also are manipulated by the mass media. Strong public or audience dependence on media for information, education, and entertainment, though extensively used by Western media experts and practiced in developed societies, is not seen in Cameroon because it is a newly independent nation-state with relatively young media. Thus Cameroon's emphasis is on the dissemination of messages that promote unity and patriotism — both "development" constructs. A major purpose of the media is to disseminate development information. Cameroon journalist Bandolo (1985) said that the national press cannot and does not support any action that negates national unity (p. 223). The concept of national unity implies complete support on issues of democratization, civic responsibility, and change by all Cameroonians, irrespective of their ethnic background, education or cultural values. In 1984, Information Minister Sengat Kuo cautioned that uncontrolled information could disturb public order and hurt state security. The implication of this statement is that uncensored information would be very costly to the citizens and to the state. However, democracy implies that people have the right to receive, accept, or reject information, question its sources and behave at will toward its content.

The concept of the freedom to choose and act stems from the policymaker's stance that information should reflect facts about the country and provide a collective and unifying spirit among the citizens. Information must "inform and educate at home," asserts former Cameroon President Ahidjo (1968). The news media in Cameroon should provide information for their citizens, since the absence or inadequacy of information may lead to a passive and less informed people. Information that demands change, unity and development is important, especially for rural people whose needs are not being addressed in the government's development agenda.

An analysis of the pronouncements of Cameroon's political leaders and media personnel indicates that there is no use of public opinion in determining the media agenda and government policy on major development issues. Rural people's opinions of change are not considered as media programs are developed. The people are not motivated to participate in the democratic and civil activities that are important in developing the country. It is clear that the contribution of electronic and traditional mass media to the development of Cameroon is underused and ineffective to date.

Among the major issues addressed by this book:

* The potential use of the mass media in rural development in Africa.
* The effectiveness of the use of TV and radio for development purposes in rural areas in Cameroon since 1972.
* The perception of Cameroon broadcast media by rural residents and government officials.
* The content of information broadcast to rural people through radio and TV programs, and the type and frequency of the programs broadcast between 1972 and 1994.
* The correlation between the information sent and the opinions of rural residents.

This book evaluates the extent to which rural people believe that the broadcast and traditional media have assisted rural development. The text also examines which type of media rural residents feel can and should disseminate development information: electronic mass media or traditional mass media. As a road map for the investigation, the following issues will be addressed:

1. What was the role of the Cameroonian media in rural development between 1972 and 1994?
2. What was the mandate given to the Cameroon media by the government regarding their role in rural development and national integration?
3. To what extent have the media fulfilled the terms of the mandate?
4. How do rural Cameroonians and government officials perceive the role of the broadcast media in rural development in Cameroon?

This book provides socioeconomic information on the factors that contribute to unproductive community activity, more poverty in the African village, heavy dependence on government, and idleness.

More than 170,000 Cameroon citizens are employed by the government. The majority of them live in the urban areas, according to the 1991 chief officer of the economic division of the Cameroon Embassy in Washington, D.C. The officer also revealed that the World Bank asked the Cameroon government to reduce the number of government employees in order to enhance the management of human resources and reduce government expenses.

Since so many Cameroonians rely on the government for employment, and most government offices operate in urban areas, the focus of government efforts has for several years been on urban development, as shown in Tables 1.1 and 1.2. Cameroon, for example, was one of the world's largest producers of cocoa, bananas and coffee in the early 1980s. Over 500 foreign business organizations operated in Cameroon in the 1970s and 1980s in addition to over 5,000 indigenous businesses. Since Cameroon's economic crisis intensified in 1986, many government jobs have been eliminated and unemployment has increased. It is important therefore, to study what will best assist the rural people to develop their communities and provide a thriving, productive agricultural base.

Rural communities in Cameroon have rich natural resources, manpower and skills, valuable values and philosophies, creative abilities, and other resources for development that have not been tapped because of a lack of communication among government, media and rural people. According to the 1987 Ministry of Information and culture report, most of the population is rural and poor and does not have access to electronic media or knowledge of media languages. Out of 6,000,000 francs (CFA) budgeted in 1985-86 for development projects, only 26.1% of that amount was allocated for the rural sector, as opposed to 67.1% for secondary education (Ministry of Planning and Territorial Administration, 1986). The financial attention given to the development of rural economy and/ or investment has fluctuated since 1981, and this unpredictable assistance has caused rural people's living standards in Cameroon to fluctuate as well. It is unclear what government intentions toward rural welfare are. One wonders if government members:

- Support rural change, and
- Encourage the use of such mass traditional media as songs, town-criers, market sessions, village gatherings, popular theater, group discussions, and other folk media that can motivate, educate, and mobilize the rural masses.

Table 1.1

Distribution of funds for economic development according to sector (in thousand million francs)

Sector	1981-82	1982-83	1983-84
Rural Development	13.8	45.1	27.7
Industry SMU Handicraft	16.5	5.3	---
Mines and Power	3.5	4.2	5.8
Trade and Transport	14.2	19.6	21.6
Tourism and Hotel	0.6	2.9	1.5
Community Infrastructure	17.4	53.4	34.0
Youth and Sports	0.2	---	0.1
Education and Training	2.3	12.7	2.7
Information and Culture	1.2	8.1	1.9
Health and Social Affairs	---	0.3	5.3
Town Planning & Housing Regional Development	12.0	16.7	4.0
Administrative Facilities	62.3	31.5	22.9
Studies and Research	---	1.2	---
Total	144.0	201.0	127.5

(Source: Ministry of Finance/Ministry of Planning and Territorial Administration (1986). *VIth-Five Year Development Plan 1986-1991 p.* 26. Republic of Cameroon)

Table 1.2
Distribution of public investment credits during the implementation of the fifth Five-Year Development Plan (in thousand million francs)

	1981 - 1982		1982 - 1983		1983 - 1984	
Sector	Amt.	%	Amt.	%	Amt.	%
Rural Development	70.1	13.2	129.7	17.7	82.4	12.4
Industry SMU Handicraft	128.7	24.2	171.5	23.3	127.6	19.2
Mines and Power	22.3	4.2	14.5	2.0	20.1	3.0
Trade and Transport	31.6	5.9	31.3	4.2	5.4	8.8
Tourism and Hotel Trade	1.7	0.3	5.5	0.8	46.3	7.0
Community Infrastructure	84.4	15.8	156.7	21.3	116.7	17.5
Education and Training	10.0	1.9	51.9	7.1	18.8	2.8
Youth and Sports	1.5	0.3	1.6	0.2	1.6	0.2
Information and Culture	1.9	0.4	27.3	3.7	4.4	0.7
Health and Social Affairs	4.1	0.8	6.7	0.9	18.2	2.7
Town Planning and Housing Regional Dev.	36.8	6.9	32	4.4	72	10.8
Administrative Facilities	104.9	19.7	69.7	9.5	48.6	7.3
Studies and Research	7.9	1.5	6.0	0.8	4.5	0.7
Inv./Rel Debts	26.0	4.9	30.0	4.1	46.0	6.9
Total	531.6	100.0	734.4	100.0	665.6	100.0

Source: Ministries of Finance & Planning & Territorial Admn. 1986. *VIth Five Year Development Plan 1986-1991* p.25). Cameroon.

Apart from becoming useful channels of information to the rural people, mass traditional media modes have been a part of their values for many centuries. Thus, carrying out any development programs via the electronic media requires media planners' understanding of ethnic groups' values. Although electronic mass media have been used in such developing countries as Tanzania, Swaziland, Nicaragua, and Puerto Rico to awaken rural consciousness of health care, family planning, and nutritional facilities, the success has not been overwhelming; neither has it lasted long. The supposed reason for this limited success is that the value of rural people's *modus operandi* was underestimated.

Desired change in behavior disseminated through mass media among a people with a strong cultural foundation cannot be adequately realized if the people's indigenous communication values and other social indices are not understood and used optimally by the agents of development.

There is no significant rural development when communication researchers, media planners, and major policymakers remain ignorant of government's version of such development. The indigenes of any society should be responsible for the changes that take place there. Africa's development lies in the hands of Africans. Obviously, it is politically disadvantageous for foreign powers to provide solutions to the problems of rural livelihood in Africa because most of these powers do not operate in that locale. African people, scholars, developers, major policymakers, and researchers should *Africentricize* concepts and agendas for their own development.

Todaro (1976) documents that most urban migrants in Third World countries "tend to be single males between the ages of 15 and 25" (p. 27). The villages are abandoned to children and the aging, whose strength is insufficient to undertake domestic and/or economic chores like gardening, farming, transporting, and cleaning their surroundings. The ultimate effects on the psychophysical condition of village people and rural infrastructure are great. Migrating to urban centers leads to laziness, hunger, more poverty, more vulnerability to diseases, and heavier dependence on foreign aid.

Village authorities can reduce practices that obstruct rural development if they seek the advice of researchers familiar with rural lifestyle. A widespread campaign for self- and collective improvement can become effective with use of the mass communication media. To accomplish that goal, a firm knowledge of Africentricity is required by policymakers and researchers alike.

Africentric scholars like Asante (1987), and Carruthers and Karenga (1986) have called on African scholars to operate from an African worldview. Using the same conceptual framework, Nwanko and M'Bayo (1989, p. 12) posit that African scholars and "sympathizers of African aspirations" should endeavor to "develop an African ideology" as their bedrock policy for defining development. Other scholars are asking for a synchronization of African traditions as a way of gaining control over African resources.

Pan-Africanist scholar Kwame Nkrumah said that African leaders should realize that mass communication can accelerate the pace of change in African countries (Nkrumah, 1964). Even Cameroon government officials have stressed the importance of using the mass media in expediting national development. In what he called "freedom of undertaking" (Biya, 1987, pp. 116-122), and in many interviews with the government-sponsored media, the president has emphasized that the media of mass communication in Cameroon should serve as mediators between and increase interaction among Cameroonians:

> The role of the Cameroon press within the country should be to contribute to the emancipation and well-being of the Cameroonian so that he can live as a free and mature citizen who is aware of his political, civic and social responsibilities *(Cameroon Tribune,* July 6, 1984).

The media of communication bear testimony to Cameroon's new role in the global community and contribute to the projection of Cameroon's image (Matip, 1985). Because of their ability to reach and influence the behavior and thought of many people, the media of communication are realistic agents of development.

Based on the above, this study will address two major factors in media and politics: theories of media effects and indices of national development. Some researchers have found that mass media content influences viewers' perceptions and decisions (Rubin and Perse, 1989, pp. 55-57). However, those not exposed to media content but who are associated with exposed viewers also become influenced through hearsay. Political campaigns in Cameroonian towns are heavily attended by non-English and non-French speaking audiences. The 1993 Secretary General of the SDF party, has remarked that supporters of his party get more information about the government in power through the interpretations of major officials in his party than through government-owned radio and television. Although the electronic media also cover international issues, they disseminate very limited information.

In his book on communal liberalism, Biya (1987) asks policymakers to be open-minded and receptive to ideas that change the society. Berrigan (1977) recommends that each country have a policy making and planning organization that considers alternative measures in resolving development problems (p. 21). values and behavioral patterns of the masses are the foundations of a nation's development. People's values and attitudes change through absorbing the content of electronic media messages and through intrapersonal interactions. This book also explores the educated use of values and traditions to determine the extent to which rural people foresee improving their lot.

Other scholars have raised underlying development concepts of communication that apparently stem from the premise that positive change in Third World countries should begin with holistic development or development from the grassroots. These grassroots are the rural areas that harbor most of the people in the continent. Many Africanist scholars introduce an agenda-setting theory for Africa's development. Ugboajah (1985) for example, calls on researchers to document indigenous media and reassess their own techniques on the role of communication in national development.

There can be no development of an African ideology nor synchronization of cultures without a systematic understanding of indigenous cultures, values, and beliefs.

The theory of African autonomy posits that research on Third World communication studies should not look only at information diffusion problems. If Third World governments develop and implement public education programs on a continuous basis, the quality of life in the rural areas will improve. Ethnic communities in Africa should reassess their cultural paradigms in order to develop a resourceful agenda for development. Talents and skills hidden among rural people, when detected, could reduce African governments' dependence on foreign cultures. To accomplish this, researchers should continue dialogues with multiethnic groups and spend more time in the villages to determine if rural people would articulate rural development messages better when the latter are broadcast on the mass media. The urgency of these issues and the need to address them immediately are predicated upon the fact that the rural people suffer the most from the current economic crisis in Cameroon.

Students, communication practitioners, technical assistance agencies, and policymakers will benefit from using this book. It encourages the application of both electronic and traditional mass media channels in disseminating development information. It also describes the importance of depending on and promoting traditional mass media. The cultural integrity of Africans has been fading away because of the presence of Portuguese, German, English, French, Swiss, and U.S. cultures during the past four centuries. Asking rural people about their use of traditional media forms may motivate them to use media channels to improve the quality of their lives. Since rural villages are separated by such geophysical parameters as rivers and mountains, traditional forms of communication may not suffice to unify a country. Using electronic media channels to supplement town criers, village gatherings, and other traditional mass media forms would expedite and motivate a change in rural people's attitudes toward health care and other practices.

Due to the social and economic crises currently plaguing Africa, it is important to study rural people's perceptions of the feasibility of developing and disseminating rural programs, as rural people operate in a communal way. Rural communities in Cameroon have tremendous resources like manpower, influential values, and communication abilities that have not been tapped to their benefit because of lack of effective mass communication between the government and rural masses.

Using communications for rural development enhances government-citizen relationship and brings the government closer to the rural people who deserve more attention, since they have the resources the country needs to develop fully.

The importance of the media of communication, especially the broadcast media, is reflected in Cameroon's investments in obtaining, processing and distributing messages for Cameroonians. The broadcast media should assist government in promoting social, economic, educational, and cultural programs. This book analyzes the extent to which those objectives have been met by the media.

In order to understand the perceptions of the Cameroon people, we will examine the political history of the state. A critical account of the precolonial, colonial and postcolonial cultures in Cameroon helps the reader to understand the geoethnic landscape in which communication and rural development in Cameroon operated prior to 1972 and from which researchers and media planners can advance better theories on the rural indigenes' ideas and perceptions of development. Explaining the political and cultural history of Cameroon throws some light on the ways in which colonial administration might have affected the interpersonal behavior of village people in Cameroon and their views on administration in independent Cameroon.

The study has used a descriptive/analytical method. A description of these issues entails analyzing mass media contributions to rural development in the past and present, and speculating about their future roles. The following specific procedures were used:

- A content analysis of programs disseminated through Cameroon radio and television to determine how much information on rural development is featured. The programs analyzed came from the national radio and TV stations in Yaoundé, the nation's capital, and Bamenda, a provincial capital because they broadcast information for the provincial geoethnic groups. A sample of program logs the provincial radio and the national radio-TV station across 22 years (1972-1994) is included, to show the presence or absence of rural-oriented programs in broadcasts of stations with large audiences.

- A survey study comprising face-to-face interviews, using two interview schedules — one for government officials in the areas of information, culture, and territorial planning, and the other for villagers, is also carried out.

Defining Some Development Terms

It is difficult to define terms, since they carry different meanings. Terms like change, communication, democratization, effectiveness and information have analogous meanings but remain encapsulated in the framework of development communication.

Change refers to that which happens in time and space. Change will be seen in the context of this study as the idea of affecting people's values, opinions, beliefs, and attitudes for the purpose of unifying, integrating, and improving people's lives in the rural areas of the nation. In this study, the process of change is based on individual and societal activities. In terms of individual practices, the study looks at the implications of traditional and electronic communications in improving the living standards of rural people in Cameroon. The Marxist concept that change is a social process fits into the praxis of this study. A Cameroonian educator summarizes the concept of change as it pertains to Cameroon. The scholar sees change in Cameroon as:

an amalgam of peoples, languages, and cultures; a panorama of natural landscapes, successive colonial administrations and educational backgrounds.... Cameroon is forging a nation, a people and a nationality by the many but peaceful changes. Cameroonians are driving or hope to be driving toward an ideal: one nation, united, peaceful and prosperous (Ejedepang-Koge, 1985, p. xii).

Change as process involves persuading citizens to think and behave differently for the benefit of the entire village and/or nation. Tsurutani (1 973) adds:

> the process of national development involves change in values and behavior which, in turn, translates itself into the emergence of new patterns of expectation on the part of various groups in society toward the kind and level of government performance (Tsurutani,1973, p. 109).

Change is used invariably in this study to mean development.

Communications refers to the process of making information and ideas common and available to people of all socioeconomic and cultural backgrounds. It is also a social process, a means, or a technology. Communication can be studied in the context of economic growth, education, political mobilization or immobilization, revolution, literacy reform, or sociocultural behavior. People should share and understand by communicating. *Communications* also refers to the availability and use of precolonial channels of interacting like drums, guns, theaters, public gatherings, town criers, gossip, word of mouth and postcolonial media like TV and radio. *Communications* is used in this study as both an ideological and a performance entity.

Development refers to the ways in which a society optimally exploits and manages its resources. Some African policymakers define development to suit their agenda. The Cameroon government evaluates development through Congress sessions that take place once every five years. The Sixth Five-Year Development Planning Committee, which met to decide development strategies for Cameroon from 1986 to 1991, resolved that planned liberalism, self-reliance, social justice and balanced development would be the indices for national development. The planning committee also mentioned rural development (Ministry of Information and culture, 1986, p. 34).

Scholarly definitions differ according to the researcher's cultural and educational background. In his book *How Europe Underdeveloped Africa*, Rodney sees development as increased skill and capacity, greater freedom, self-discipline, creativity, responsibility and material well-being (1982, p. 3).

From a performance perspective, development entails having a mind free to think and operate toward the betterment of the individual and his or her immediate environment. Its paradigms include more and better health care activities, a reduction of disease opportunities, growing more food to curb hunger, and changing personal attitudes, opinions, values, and beliefs to encompass the feelings and expectations of others. The process of development should include constructive and interactive activities of an individual or a group of people. One development theorist provides five fitting characteristics of development. Langer (1979) states that development is significant when:

1. An individual interacts with his or her environment to reach a new level;
2. An individual or a group of people conserve that interaction,
3. The group of people introduces new systems of action to enable individuals to become more adaptive,
4. Interactions lead to more systems of functioning within the community, and
5. Interactions evoke self-adaptation (Langer, 1979, p. 279).

But how can one begin to evaluate development in Africa objectively? Through Rodney's philosophy, or Langer's, or both? To do this effectively, an evaluator must understand Africa's sociocultural values. Alienating African rural residents from the so-called development agendas, most rural-oriented programs do not stand the test of time. In the 1970s, villagers in Tanzania did not know of the existence of a nation or the institution of the President when their own head of state, Julius Nyerere, visited them. Righter (1978) says that the villagers had never been reached by the mass media. This implies that development strategists and media planners failed to give priority to village residents. Wagao (1992) concurs, but points out that the number of indigenous cadres with managerial, technical, financial, and administrative experience increased between 1962 and 1970. Tanzania has since made significant economic progress through multi media campaigns and increased worker-farmer participation. However, the situation is not the same in other African countries. According to Boafo (1978, p. 15), information policies in sub-public gatherings to community work. The term *rural* is often replaced by *village.*

Rural-oriented messages refers to information for and about people in the village community.

National Development is the process whereby a politically, socially and economically integrated society checks its built-in capacities for continuous growth or progress and adaptation among its citizens (Tsurutani, 1973, p. 179). Tsurutani adds that government regularizes processes and methods to resolve conflict and to optimize change. That line of thought presupposes that a faction of the population takes the initiative to develop procedures that monitor evolutionary changes and to effect compromise between the people's demands and levels of integrity. The latter approach looks to the institutionalization of communicative messages and programs that promote self-creativity, self-adaptation and progressive change.

Chapter Two contains a description of the rural African environment and identifies potential resources for development. It also highlights some folk media Chapter.

Chapter Three provides a critical examination of Cameroon's historical and political landscape. It looks at the origin of its inhabitants, the geoethnic and political diversities of its cultural groups, and its traditional and colonial governments to help determine the atmosphere in which communication and rural development in Cameroon have operated and from which one can better understand the fundamental views of indigenous Cameroonians, especially village people, before formulating appropriate development theories. It further throws some light on the geohistorical, administrative and cultural behavior of some Saharan African countries have not adequately dealt with the application of modern communication technologies. Thus, socioeconomic development problems prevail because of a lack of proper communication policies and activities to support development efforts.

Development communications refers to the use of the mass media to support and promote social and economic activities in the rural sectors. Can communication and development be used interchangeably as psychosociological and performance entities? Can communication cause development? Mowlana (1993b) has argued that communication does not cause development; rather, both evolve concomitantly toward new political, social and economic institutions (pp. 3-9). The concept of new is equitable with *change* or *progress.* Thus, communication systems, as well as social, political and economic situations, can change as time passes. The use of electronic and non-electronic media to motivate, stimulate, educate and mobilize one or more target groups to respond to change in health, education, agriculture, nutrition, family planning and other socioeconomic and political practices can be described as development communications. Broadcast and traditional media forms like radio, TV, and theaters, gossip, and public gatherings are applied in order to:

- Achieve educational objectives,
- Acquire information, and
- Motivate the rural masses to be more committed, evaluative, and integrative toward government support programs and toward their own collective daily activities.

Democratization is a term frequently used by major African politicians, policymakers and Cameroon's 1994 President to denote a sense of nationhood or commitment to national values. The leadership in Cameroon sees *democratization* as the "clear demonstration of an exemplary sense of responsibility" (Ministry of Information and culture, 1985, p. 12). Democratization implies frank cooperation and full participation of the people in expressing their needs (Biya, 1987, p. 59). Democratization can be further defined as the practice of full dignity and a high standard of undisputed unity and pride in the fatherland.

By *effectiveness* is meant the quantity and quality of rural-oriented messages sent to the rural people through the broadcast media and the amount of messages received by a target audience. Effectiveness is also the ability to transmit rural development messages to the rural public within the shortest and most appropriate time. In this book, effectiveness will not be considered from a strictly experimental (pretest/ post-test) perspective, but as a totally descriptive construct. An overall description of the perceptions of rural people and officials in the government on the performance of communications media in Cameroon in disseminating information for rural development is also provided.

Information is an ideology or a vehicle used to shape feelings and decisions. In this study, it refers to messages disseminated through radio, TV, folklore, town criers, village gatherings, and other local media of communication, as well as programs. Information on radio and TV is disseminated mostly in French and English, while local languages are seldom used.

Rural refers to the lives led by people in the countryside. Their habits include reverence toward the pasture, belief in myth, and activities that involve everyone in the village community. Such activities range from birth and death celebrations, herbal medical practice, and occasional traditional societies to show how those factors might have affected their group behavior.

Chapter Four reviews literature on the subject. Theoretical perspectives on communication and development and case studies of communications supporting rural development in certain Third World countries are reviewed. The chapter discusses the negative influence of dependency on Third World policies and administration. It describes certain forms of communication that have been used in supporting rural development today and explains how and why they were used in the village community prior to colonial administration in Cameroon.

Chapter Five is a description of methodology divided into three sections: historico-critical approach, content analysis, and survey research. It describes some of the electronic and traditional forms of communication used in the survey study.

In Chapter Six, the data collected are discussed and the findings reported. It also contains a summary of the findings and conclusions.

Chapter Seven consists of suggestions and recommendations based on findings and the discussion of similar case studies.

CHAPTER 2

THE RURAL AFRICAN WORLD

Rurality is usually associated with primitiveness and backwardness. It implies agrarian, old-fashioned, nonmodern, lacking in technology, etc. Rural people are generally considered to have limited or no knowledge of any world other than their own geophysical environment or any values other than those they live by. Thus, no matter how strange and parochial their beliefs, or how provincial their milieu, they rarely migrate to a nonrural environment except when their world view has been influenced by city-dwellers.

Rural people migrate to the cities in search of better economic standards. According to Caldwell (1969), Todaro (1976), and Devereux (1993), young people move to the cities to look for employment and to become more successful traders. However, some of them commute to the villages and/or towns to purchase and sell perishable and non perishable products for a profit. Such major African cities as Douala, Onitsha, Lagos, Nairobi, Dakar, Cape Town, Abidjan, and Addis Ababa are congested with unemployed, uneducated and undertrained young people.

The influx into the congested townships and difficulty in finding jobs make a case for the creation and self-management of rural-oriented programs. A lack of modern technology in rural areas does not and should not prevent rural residents from augmenting their quality of life.

The rural areas of Africa have rich resources, from untapped minerals to undertapped human potential. For centuries, African villages have survived intertribal wars, harsh weather and interpersonal conflicts. The villagers have upheld the customs passed on from their ancestors through folklore. They still maintain traditional values and attitudes toward marriage, funeral and birth rites, and other group activities. Their legal systems and such institutions as open-air story telling and circumcision centers, local psychics, market places, prophets, masquerades, political leaders, and rhetoricians provide incentives for the cultivation of ideas.

Why should others seek to replace those information sources with sophisticated electronic and telecommunication technology when the former agents are cheaper, familiar to village people, and hence easier to manage? What providers of electronic information appliances fail to realize is that rural residents are capable of governing themselves and managing their environment better than anyone else, especially when they motivate themselves or are motivated to design and manage their own programs. Development planners, researchers, scholars, policymakers and international development agencies like UNESCO, UNDP, UNICEF, the World Bank, USIA, IMF, and the Peace Corps apply the show-them-how-to-do-it approach. They mainly design and implement programs in rural areas without incorporating the residents' values or understanding what rural people know and what they can do.

Although some programmers have succeeded in using media campaigns to educate people on certain health and social issues, the success did not last, for the following reasons: funds for the programs ran out, and the programs were carried out only periodically. This on-and-off process makes an objective evaluation of development programs difficult.

Development should be a continuous process. Information regarding development projects and target audiences should be in constant circulation within the cycle of policymakers, media planners, project sponsors and target audiences. There should be a constant cycle of input and feedback among the target audiences and the aforenamed entities. Before anything else, however, the policymakers, media planners and project sponsors must understand the psychosocial composition of the population being targeted for development.

Categories of Rural Residents

The rural African usually has three types of social consciousness; the remote conscience, the split psyche, and the contemporary personality.

The *remote conscience* steadfastly maintains and performs ancestral rituals. Such a person sees the village landscape and its people as sacred structures. He is very reverent toward fauna, flora and the cosmos. He spends his life only in the place of his birth or in another village that follows the same customs. He thinks in and speaks mainly his mother tongue. He recognizes and worships every aspect of his people's tradition. His mindset cannot be influenced by a foreign school of thought; he observes and accepts things at their face value but never chooses to participate in major decisionmaking—that is, decisions affecting other villagers. He is usually kind and stoical toward strangers and opts to help as soon as he establishes communication with the stranger. He is often inclined to acting rather than reacting. His behavior is orthodox. He has only some basic economic amenities to take him through the day.

Even in the modern era, this caliber of village resident still strongly adheres to ancestral values. The mentality of the rural resident virtually blocks his ability to absorb other values—unless they have supernatural aspects. His chief socioeconomic activities include subsistence farming, livestock-rearing, hunting, bush-burning, and attending and actively participating in all public activities except those which traditional laws prohibit.

This class of people is diminishing rapidly in African villages because of the forceful infiltration of foreign culture and its emphasis on individual economic advancement. Villagers are being influenced through the messages they receive from users of electronic media, through interacting with missionaries, through their children's attending public schools, and through the marketplace, where they meet food buyers from the townships.

The *split psyche* loves ancestral values as well, but he yearns to sample certain aspects of foreign customs. He thinks, chooses, and often questions "negative" cultural attributes. He likes foreign music, dress codes, food, language, and lovemaking techniques. He yearns to interact with foreigners and receive foreign instruction or education. Part of his life is spent in the township.

Certain members of this group have strong links with powerful village members, such as chiefs, heirs, and family heads. Some of them uphold both traditional and modern values, in order to benefit from both economically and socially. A village teacher trained in the European tradition earns more money than a local blacksmith, and thus gets more respect from the people.

This category of village residents consists of young men and women aged 18 to 40 years, a rapidly increasing caste. The split psyche is often a traditional Euro-modern teacher or a small-scale farmer who sells household paraphernalia and often makes a small profit. He attends both traditional gatherings and Christian churches. He may run a liquor store, where he comes in contact with foreigners who influence his native consciousness.

The *contemporary personality* is in the process of abandoning indigenous values and embracing contemporary ones. Although he often lives in the village, he prefers to be in the cities to improve his economic standard. He attends local parties where foreign, especially Western music is played, and he strives to speak European languages in a cosmopolitan manner, even when interacting with his fellow village folk. He tends to question and reject most local values. This group includes mostly young traders, schoolteachers, storekeepers, hospital workers, clerks and government workers.

Folk Media Types and Their Potential

The Interpersonal Model

The psyche of the typical rural African is intertwined with primitive notions of existence. Such a person, who strongly believes in a cosmogony, virtually surrenders his intuition to providence. According to Bois (1968), this is how the primitive villager views himself in the world:

> I am in a world ruled by the gods.
> I must become acquainted with the gods.
> I must find their designs on the world and on me.
> I must appease them with offerings, sacrifices and rituals.
> I must curry their favor and keep them on my side.
> My agents to deal with the gods are the Sybil, the Oracle, the Magicians, the Shamans, and the priests (1968, p. 4).

Understanding the world views of rural people is fundamental for understanding different ways of preparing and spreading rural development messages to suit their needs. Rural people can also help media planners, development agencies, and policymakers to determine which media to use in spreading the information. The split psyche and contemporary personalities — whose members are increasing, due in part to the lengthy influence of colonial administrators and the heavy way flow of Western values into the rural areas through Peace Corps and other foreign personnel working there, and through books, magazines, vehicles, newspapers, radio sets, cameras, videotaped programs, and other forms of Western technology and satellite systems—would be efficient in spreading development messages. After all, these forms can reach mass audiences much faster than folk media.

Better communication takes place through face-to-face contact. The village whose space is about one square mile is a compact unit wherein frequent and intensive communication takes place. It is small, in geographical terms, and densely populated; it comprises many human groups with common values. Family ties are close, and interfamily relations are strong. In most African villages, a son or daughter may marry a neighbor; they may choose to live with the groom's or bride's family or start their own family on an uninhabited piece of land. Unless there is a deadly epidemic, families increase rapidly and outgrow household space. When this happens, some families migrate to the farmlands. These villagers, though somewhat removed from the stress of township life, still interact effectively with other villagers, since the villages are small.

Since rural communities in Africa are clustered, such social concepts as leadership, caste, social class, land ownership, religion, kinship, traditional medicine, religious oracles, village theatricals, marriage ties, and social gatherings can and do influence economic structures. Those geophysical and sociological elements provide a strong framework for healthy communication and economic growth. In his study of rural groups in India, Ambekar (1992) found that many families made rapid economic progress through interpersonal interaction. These families, who earned their income primarily through farming, increased their land acreage for the rearing of hens, goats, cows, buffaloes, and other livestock. They were usually of a royal caste.

The caste structure is also a medium of communication because ideas originate in one group and reach other groups. Some ideas are distilled before they are delivered, to suit the scope and functional needs of both the deliverers and the receivers. Ambekar found that ideas originated from high caste members and were distilled for middle caste members (1992, p. 20). In rural communities of Cameroon, Nigeria, and Ghana, information production and dissemination flows three ways: among the high, intermediate, and regular castes. The high caste comprises the monarchy (king, queen, clan head). The intermediate group in some African rural communities comprises quarter/village leaders and chiefs and other local administrators, who have been appointed by the king. The intermediate group also includes an heir or heiress. The regular class includes children, young people, and older ones without titles. A married man with one or two wives and no traditional title or wealth also belongs to this caste. Depending on its degree of importance to the people, information originates from the king's residence and passes through the intermediate authorities to the regular villager. Serious complaints, disputes and other concerns of personal or group interest are channeled to the king through village heads or chiefs only when this intermediate caste cannot resolve them internally (see Figure 2.1).

Figure 2.1
Problem-solving and policymaking in traditional communities

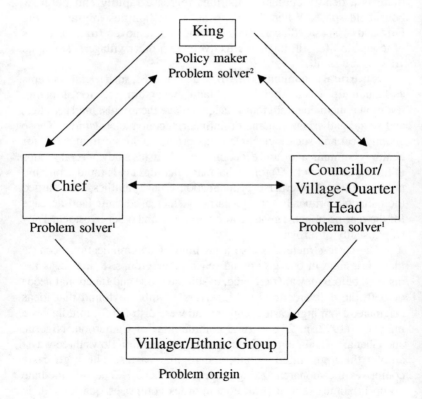

Communication factors in rural areas in Africa include caste, numerical dominance, traditional leadership, public gatherings, drama, flutes, drums, the family, village bus terminals, mosques and churches. The list is inexhaustible. A brief description of some of these variables follows.

Numerical Dominance

There is extensive communication among dominant groups in many regions. Every *ndichie* (in general terms, an important person or title holder among the Igbo in Nigeria. Formerly used to mean a wise deceased person or ancestor) or local dignitary who is known for his religious, political, or economic influence interacts extensively with other villagers because they approach him for assistance. Although he sometimes communicates with them through his valet or *nchindo* (Kom), their influx into his homestead in search of financial assistance or advice cannot be stopped. Visiting is a strong value among villagers in Sub-Saharan Africa. The socioeconomic and political status of dominant group individuals both requires and permits frequent interaction. Butchers, goat-herders, livestock farmers, buyers and sellers in African villages interact frequently with each other at the market place, farm, or grazing ground.

The numerical dominance of the Muslims, the Hausa and Yoruba in Nigeria, the Bamiléké in Cameroon, the Hutus in Rwanda and Burundi, the Ovimbundu in Angola, the Ndebele in Zimbabwe, and the Gikuyu (who have migrated to other regions in Kenya but who dominate economically), accounts for the homogeneity in their communities. There are also other politically and economically dominant groups like the Baule of Ivory Coast, who were the ruling class during President Houphouet Boigny's regime; the Kongo and Luba in Zaire; the Wolof in Niger, Mauritania, Gambia and Senegal; and the Zulu and Xhosa in South Africa. There must be a degree of interpersonal communication among the Zulu who make up 7,000,000 of the total population of about 29,000,000 South Africans. Their high degree of interaction has given them political solidarity and enabled them to fight against and defeat the apartheid regimes there. Although the Inkatha Freedom Party is a minority political group in the Zulu tribe, there is a high degree of interaction between its members because they share the same political ideology.

Since northern Africa has been mostly ignored by scholars writing in the Anglo-Saxon idiom, one may be tempted to overlook the communication forms that have helped to maintain unity among the Arab nations. Although no tribes or groups dominate numerically, there is a high degree of personal and interpersonal communication in Libya, Morocco, Algeria and Tunisia, due in part to the bond of a common language — Arabic — and a common religion — Islam. Muslims are highly spiritual. In addition, newspapers like *Al-Aram* , an international paper headquartered in Cairo, Egypt, and distributed in the Middle East, and other print media circulate information in Arabic.

It is also safe to say that any group, no matter what its size, has a considerable degree of communication and circulates information for the benefit of its members. For example, the Bamiléké, who control the economy of Cameroon, circulate much of Cameroon's currency among themselves. They have many large cooperative societies where they deposit money and obtain business loans to construct buildings for business, purchase public transportation vehicles, or manage major retail stores in the country. The majority of Cameroon currency is reportedly deposited in French banks by Bamiléké businessmen and businesswomen. Although they no longer have political control since they lost the civil war to the Ahidjo regime in the 1960s, the Bamiléké, who consider each other as *famille*, have regrouped through the use of one indigenous language spoken all over the region. There are also frequent interactions between members of *FAMLAH*, an influential sacred society of many Bamiléké people.

A numerically dominant group can exchange development ideas because of intensive interaction among its members.

Traditional Leadership

The role of the village leader is very important. He is the focal point of the village, hence the news source in the village communication system, as stated earlier (see Figure 2.2). This focal role of the village ruler has a genealogical tradition, filled with domination. In the Kom kingdom, there are the *nchisendo* — king's valets, who work as servants and messengers in the kingdom's head quarters, Laikom. Ritual specialists, powerful medicine men (native doctors), and soothsayers assist the king in maintaining peace and in spreading vital information to everyone in the kingdom.

The village head enjoys fewer privileges than the king, but he still has considerable influence over the people. Blacksmiths, carpenters, local farmers, and small-scale businessmen and businesswomen visit the village headquarters to offer gifts and chat. During annual festivals, they may also negotiate their problems and needs with the gift receiver, the village head.

Figure 2.2
News source in the village

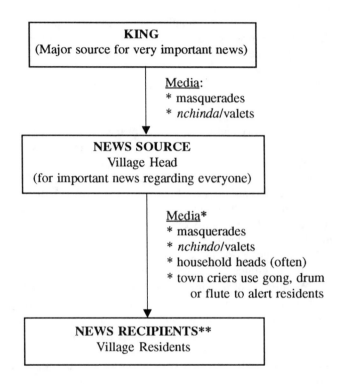

*These transmitters usually go around the village at night when most people are at home. They do not process the news. They only report.

**Village residents can send querries/messages to the King through the Village Head

The village head's resolutions of land disputes and other local problems are usually final, except when he takes the problem to the king's court. Rarely do villagers settle interpersonal problems by themselves or take their cases to a national court of law. The villager's belief in the absolute power of their leader makes them more united. This unity reduces delays and problems that could have arisen if the village were divided by factions.

A unidirectional information pattern can be helpful in disseminating development messages in African villages, since most village residents still respect the office of the traditional ruler.

Caste, Wealth, Song, and Burial Grounds

In many African villages, people are judged by their contributions to social stability and to the growth of the society. A wealthy person — that is, an individual who has many goats, cows, pigs, fowls, farms, wives, children, and houses — receives a more respectable burial than someone of lower status. In the Akan community in Ghana, and as depicted in this author's book, *Dawn in Rage* (1992), the social group is an important ingredient in awarding respect. People of lower status are stoical toward the wealthy ones. A wealthy person is deemed correct in just about everything he says or does. Kingly status is contingent not only upon hard work and success but also upon wealth. Thus, wealth in the African village means power and influence.

Wealthy people can use their socioeconomic influence to disseminate vital information in the interest of everyone in the village. Village residents strive to become wealthy in order to enjoy some of the privileges associated with a kingly status. Wealth becomes not only a status symbol but also a personal communication construct. People with a high social status are potential agents for generating stamina and energy in the village.

Oratory also has cognitive significance. *Asafo* songs stress determination among the Adziwa and related groups in Ghana (Riley, 1993, pp. 253-255), and njang , a group performance song of the Kom people in Cameroon, stresses both joy and persistence. Besides the role songs play in social change, the determination to be recognized, to enjoy better privileges, or seek higher living standards constitutes development. Thinking improves human behavior; since wishful thinking can motivate positive action, it can also induce change. People working and singing simultaneously complete the work faster and properly because the melody and rhythm of the song helps them forget the stress usually attributed to work. In *Dawn in Rage* (1992), the men see work as entertainment. Thus, the singing of change-related songs should be encouraged. After all, development partly means a progressive change in ideology.

In some villages, a dignitary is buried in a sacred place apart from other people. Usually, outcasts and twins are buried next to their sibling, or on public soil, but the king is buried next to his predecessors to maintain a psychohistorical tradition. Although a common person cannot become king, no matter how hard he tries, the fact that some aspire to enjoy a similar status shows an aspiration, an effort toward achieving a goal, a need to rise above one's level and be respected by members of one's caste. That need is a worthwhile endeavor, an indication of social and moral sanity, because only a mentally ill or lazy person fails to pursue his dream/aspiration.

The Church

The number of religious individuals in African rural areas can affect the scope of interpersonal communication, either positively or negatively. According to Hoffman (1993, p. 739), out of Cameroon's population of about 12 million, 33% is Christian, and 16% Muslim. A recent catalogue of general information on Africa shows that as of 1992, one Christian organization had 147 member churches in 39 countries (Africa South of the Sahara, 1994, p. 120). That book also reveals that the Africa Conference of Churches carries out programs related to Christian unity, development, and education. Whether it hosts Christians or Muslims, and although there may be variations in numbers, the church is a powerful agent of communication. Its primary function is to promote solidarity and spirituality among its members. Most villages in sub-Saharan Africa with 1,000 or more people have a Christian church with a catechist, priest, pastor or deacon. In Northern Africa, one finds many mosques and Muslim leaders interacting. Besides promoting fellowship, these religious individuals use the holy premises to circulate information about the state of the denomination, national affairs and personal issues. The clergy in the villages offer economic and moral assistance to the villagers, and they often inculcate in them Judeo-Christian or Muslim values, beliefs and teachings. The interaction between the clergy and villagers increases steadily with an increase in mutual trust. That interactive paradigm solidifies personal, interpersonal and intergroup relations in rural areas.

Religious studies done by Father Engelbert Mveng and Ali Mazrui and reports by the All-Africa Church Conference and by Christian scholars show that villagers are increasingly converting to Christianity. Intrapersonal communication between village residents and the clergy must be effective to cause the former to convert.

As stated in Chapter One, interaction between the public and the clergy have proven successful in Eritrea and Ethiopia, where priests were used to foster an understanding between feuding political parties and to promote women's civil and voting rights. The sacred premises, the clergy, and converts can be asked to spread development messages to rural areas using flyers, sermons, demonstrations and speeches. Information on self-sustaining methods of economic growth, better health and nutritional techniques, and reduction of witchcraft and of hopeless procrastination can be disseminated through the clergy since they have a cordial relationship with the villagers. The clergy, with the support of village deacons, can spread those messages from one village house to another. There are more than 150,000,000 Christians in Africa, and since their number is expected to double by 2000 A.D. following an influx of missionaries into Africa and increased broadcasting of Western moral values to the rural areas through African electronic media, more rural development messages could be disseminated.

Physical Forms of Communication

Clothes and Other Sartorial Constructs

Traditional physical forms of communication are mainly art, fabrics and other things that people see and use. They can be less helpful in transmitting development messages in the global village than oral forms, because they communicate through signs and, as such, different signs and signals would communicate different messages to different ethnic groups. Thus, physical forms can only be used among the villagers familiar with them.

Among some Bantu in Cameroon, a hairless head and/or white piece of cloth tied around a wrist or head shows that family members are in mourning. In Cameroon and elsewhere, a red feather on a hat is a marker of high class in society; it shows that the wearer is a dignitary in the tribe and must be respected. Different cloth designs among the Akan and Ashanti of Ghana, the Igbo and Yoruba of Nigeria, the Bamiléké of Cameroon, etc., have different meanings. Men and women send messages by wrapping a piece of cloth or wearing a head scarf in a particular way. Among Nigerian and Ghanaian women, hairstyle indicates whether the individual is available or married. Some Yoruba women wear damasks designed with the picture of a Mercedes Benz. Vogel and Ebong (1991) found out that such damasks celebrate wealth. It also can show its wearer's yearning to become wealthy. The symbolism of the design suggests that people aspire to belong to the high class and yearn to be treated with respect.

Rituals

Rituals can be considered artistic forms of communication, in that people use physical forms when carrying out ritualistic activities. Nooter (1993) submits that certain kings are covered with cloth and hidden from the public when in transit. During the Odwira ritual, the king is paraded, Nooter says, through the streets at night with the knowledge of the townspeople, but in secret. The secrecy is a dramatic device to enhance the event and to increase suspense before a revelation.

The magic surrounding a king makes him a powerful element for the transmission of significant messages. With the enhancement of periodic rituals to renew his supernatural powers, the king becomes a political dramaturg who not only makes public statements about kinship but can also use his office to talk about vital issues necessary for initiating progressive change in the tribe.

Traditional sources of communication, be they oral or physical, can be used to disseminate rural development messages through careful consultation with traditional administrators and without destroying ancestral values. Traditional forms of communication can help one understand the historical lifestyle of rural residents, their caste and their world views.

This chapter has suggested that rural residents have the capacity to design and execute their own projects because they have a stable social structure and a peaceful way of living. These characteristics are useful to outsiders seeking to conceptualize development programs and messages. Programs and messages should meet the needs of rural residents. The village is not the place to implement trial programs, since rural residents have rigid, parochial views about the world. This chapter has also suggested that limited logistical and technical support are needed from outside institutions.

The next chapter further describes the historical and political landscape of an African country, sampled to indicate the climate for providing rural African communities with effective development programs and for promoting the use of appropriate communication forms and effective development messages.

CHAPTER 3

COMMUNICATING IN A HIGH-CONTEXT CULTURE

As mentioned in Chapter One, it is important to provide a brief critical analysis of the history and culture of Cameroon. No understanding of the interactions of rural residents can be reached without prior knowledge of their existence. This chapter gives a historico-cultural description of indigenous development activities carried out by various ethnic groups in Cameroon. The major reasons for describing the origins and economic activities of the groups are:

- To show that Cameroon villagers still have vestiges of their ancestral culture that can be useful in conceptualizing indigenous development issues and in communicating such issues among themselves.
- To facilitate an understanding of some of the factors that accounted for rural development crises and affected interaction among ethnic groups in the country. These factors, which are briefly examined here, include patterns of precolonial, colonial, and postcolonial administrations.

Precolonial History

The origin of Cameroon can be traced to a small village with "flint fragments" in Maroua, a town in Northern Cameroon whose inhabitants were pygmies. Before its history was recorded, that which is now the Republic of Cameroon was a conglomerate of Bantu-speaking people who dominated the plains south of the Sahara desert. They came from the coasts of Ghana and Guinea and from central and eastern Africa. The territory had an uneven diversity of social, political and economic activities. Pygmies were the first legitimate indigenes of Cameroon before Carthaginian voyager Hannon allegedly found the Cameroon mountain he called "chariot of the Gods" in the sixth century BC. Mass communication existed through business and travel. There is evidence of tremendous interaction between Cameroon indigenes and their foreign business counterparts.

> Exchanges were made in Egypt, the Fezzan, Libya, and Tchad. The Cameroon (pygmies) exported ivory, panther skins, ostrich feathers, natron, and imported pearls, bronze objects, salt, and fabrics. The crossing of the Sahara, which at that time was damp and grassy, was probably made with oxen, horses and donkeys (Ministry of Information and Culture, 1988, p. 19).

There is no written record on the specific channels of communication used by the pygmies. However, since they interacted with foreigners, they must have either spoken the same language or used nonverbal communication constructs like gestures and sign language.

An Africanist historian reports that Cameroon peoples differed notably in language and culture. Nelson (1974) states that Cameroonians "introduced a variety of traditional, social, and political systems that included egalitarian village societies, socially stratified kingdoms, and portions of vast, feudally organized empires" (p. 7).

Situated on the west coast of Africa north of the Equator, Cameroon has been seen as a crossroad for the extensive migration of many African peoples. The cultural diversity of its population reflects the variety and richness of its cultural practices. Due to the lack of written history, it is impracticable to state the origins of Cameroon peoples from an archaeological perspective. However, Cameroon's political history can be traced to the Sudan in East Africa and the Bornu, a clan that lived in Chad. The Sefua dynasty of the Sudanic clan established its power in the twelfth century AD in the Lake Region, which is now part of northern Cameroon.

The Fulani, a group that makes up about 25% of the entire Cameroonian population today, had organizational skills superior to those of other ethnic groups, which enabled them to control the northern regions of Nigeria, Lake Tchad and Northern Cameroon. Chiefdoms, kingdoms and sultanates made up the traditional administrative structure and determined the policymaking procedure of the village community. The agenda for change in the village community was set by members of those administrative units. Some administrations were autonomous, the government mostly authoritarian (see Figure 3.1).

Figure 3.1
The normal decisionmaking procedure among some precolonial tribes in Cameroon

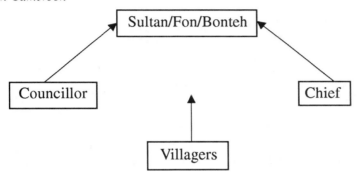

The figure also indicates that the precolonial society was socialist, in that issues affecting the lives of the indigenes were communicated to the Sultan or Fon through his councillors and chiefs. However, the leader often made decisions based on events or issues raised by the villagers. For example, an interpersonal conflict or a dispute over land ownership was resolved by the village authority or the king. There was often a healthy interactive channel between the chief, his subjects the villagers, the deity, and the king, which kept the village united and peaceful (see Figure 2.2, Chapter Two).

The channel through which social and economic matters passed made the community's problems and activities a priority on the Fon's agenda. The Sultan, Fon, or Bonteh was, in certain cases, the decisionmaker, but he made decisions after conferring with the village chiefs and councillors. In other societies, the traditional ruler was subservient to his people. He was (and is) appointed by the people to serve their interests; he can be sanctioned by his subjects. Recently, in the Menchum division of northwestern Cameroon, a king was removed from power by his subjects after having been charged with neglect of his duties. The January 3, 1994, edition of *The Herald* (a regional newspaper), reported that the king had been dismissed because of charges of forgery, lying, and belonging to a political party that his subjects did not support.

The village is governed by a Bonteh, assisted by councillors. The council is made up of ward heads, including chiefs, influential people and great achievers in the village. The communication structure was often distorted with the advent of colonial governance, causing tension among the villagers and between them, their local leaders, and the colonial administration.

The Administrative Process During the Colonial Era

Cultural Assimilation

The greatest negative influence in intervillage relations and administration was probably Dr. Zintgraff's interaction with traditional rulers in the Bamenda and Adamawa regions in the late nineteenth and early twentieth centuries.

The German explorer's policies vis-a-vis the natives discouraged friendship between them and him. It has been reported by some of his white counterparts that Zintgraff overworked but underpaid the natives (Chilver, 1966). Zintgraff frequently instructed the natives he hired to treat other natives ruthlessly. Chilver also reports that Zintgraff used the same men to raid other villages without warning. His inexperienced subordinates had so much influence over the villagers that they crippled the economy and upset the political foundations of the villages.

Acquiring power and creating disorder by bullying others in the villages and towns seems to threaten freedom of self-expression and hinder the will to act fearlessly. The natives in Cameroon villages are generally reserved toward strangers. Perhaps their docile behavior is a result of the harsh treatment their forefathers received from the voyagers. Moreover, bullying makes networking and integration difficult.

Bad roads, disease, and hunger killed most of the men traveling with Zintgraff. Such conditions forced the voyagers and their messengers to invade other villages. The invasions engendered fear, hatred, hostility, and other moral indecencies between the villages and the voyagers and led to villagers' rebellion against their local leaders. Families and political and social systems in the village communities disintegrated.

Zintgraff was a foreigner with a different skin color and a rifle. Such components of otherness constituted power and, hence, instilled fear and a feeling of loss among the indigenes. Foreigner-phobia may still have a heavy negative impact on some village residents in Africa who do not exhibit an appreciation for their own accomplishments. One can posit that the administrative processes of the French, British and Germans were geared toward destroying local administration and promoting Western culture in Cameroon. The rationale for that position lies in the desire for military advantage as well as the divide-and-rule policies practiced by colonial administrators.

Divide-and-rule, as it relates to the colonialists, can be best explained as the process whereby an administration supports and favors the privileges of one cultural group over the other. That spirit of favoritism, enhanced by their use of rifles and ammunition, betrayed the relationship between cultural groups and made them vulnerable and accessible to foreign influence and administration.

Moreover, European administrators stratified traditional chieftaincy in the village communities into three categories. According to Nelson (1974), the first category was called "First Degree Chiefs," the most powerful rulers. They served as heads of subdivisions partitioned by the colonizers. "Second Degree Chiefs" ruled groups larger than villages. "Third Degree Chiefs," who had minimal influence over the citizens, governed individual villages (Nelson, 1974). Some elderly villagers have said that chiefs of these classes received a salary from a local tax which the citizens were forced to pay. These chiefs may have given traditional political power a new meaning (Kofele-Kale, 1981).

Certain chiefs were unclassified and, therefore, powerless. Their subjects took their problems to the classified chiefs. Even the citizens were classified. Those educated in the English, French and German languages were rated superior to the "illiterate" ones by the colonial administrators.

The classification of citizens and chiefs by colonial administrators virtually nullified the powers of the Fons and Sultans and created envy and conflict among the village people. Village people began to believe that they were personae non grata because they were unable to read or write the white man's language. They began to look at those who enjoyed certain privileges with the colonial administrators as their superiors, since their own chiefs, whom they had always revered and obeyed, were now receiving governing instructions from these administrators as well.

To consolidate their power, the colonizers had to divide the tribes into smaller entities and control them. Their job was facilitated by the different languages spoken by the tribes, their differing cultural activities, and intertribal conflicts. Such problems separated the tribes rather than united them. Thus it became easier for the colonizers to penetrate the tribes and conquer them.

The most effective element of control was the colonial powers' ability to turn the cultural groups into "ethnic groups." The term "ethnic," which is frequently used to describe African cultural groups, is a biased nomenclature because it presupposes class or group conflict and tension between generations. The homogeneity and originality of indigenous African cultural groups was undermined by the infiltrators — the Europeans.

Some African and Western scholars categorize African cultural groups into holoblastic entities when they use the term "ethnic" to delineate as psychophysical the separation of these communities. Thus they can be charged with understating the stability of the precolonial African political community. If Africans continue to live as groups or clusters, it will diminish the integration of broadly based political cultures into the new nations. Although that view does not suggest the suppression of one culture in favor of the other, it can be debated. Implicit is the underlying role loyalty plays in primitive and colonized African societies. A cultural group's loyalty to its values and the desire to become loyal to the nation-state create management problems for nation's leaders because the nation may be a potpourri of traditional and foreign societies. It becomes difficult for members of a cultural group with an indigenous culture to abandon their ancestral beliefs, values, attitudes and world views and to embrace a European culture.

It seems appropriate that governments of independent African nation-states integrate the loyalties — indeed, the ideologies — of the local people into the fabric of national political culture. The progress of national political culture will remain an illusion unless cultural group loyalties are incorporated into the agendas of new nations' sociopolitical institutions.

Many Cameroon policymakers, and leaders of other nation-states, misappropriate their authority over their fellow citizens, in order to establish a homogeneous and peaceful political environment. The nation's leaders believe that it is not possible to integrate local consciousness into European principles of social and it is not possible to achieve political development without obliterating cultural group attachments to foreign leaders.

Some Cameroon policymakers got that incentive from the French, who colonized the minds of their "subjects," since they considered such colonies *la France outre-mer* (France overseas). The whole idea of la France outre-mer is to inculcate French culture into Africans in France so that they can return home and "educate" their compatriots the French way.

Cameroon's colonial administration was designed in such a way that the traditional rulers had virtually no power over their own jurisdictions. The first President of Cameroon divided the country into provinces, divisions and districts to facilitate his control. According to a former political prisoner of that regime, French administrators applied force to teach and govern Cameroonians. The indigenes who could not understand French lost many employment opportunities. Even in the highest learning institution in the country today, the Yaounde University, much instruction is given in French, and many English-speaking students drop out because they cannot communicate in French. Even the Anglo-Saxon educational system did not offer English-speaking Cameroonians much, in that the British concentrated on training secretaries for trading purposes. There was absolutely no emphasis by the colonialists on developing the rural or remote areas of the country.

Political Dynamism in Cameroon

The political climate in Cameroon has been changing since the IMF and other money-lending trust powers demanded a change in the political philosophy of African leaders. For these leaders, development means dictatorship. They use force to govern their citizens without ever incorporating the latter's demands into action. Ayittey (1992) says that 30 years of independence have yielded nothing but civil wars, famine, economic misery, flagrant violations of human rights, and repression. Ayittey (1992) describes African rulers as worse than the colonialists they replaced. Political scientist Bayart (1980, pp. 159-187), sees a contradiction between traditional political values and modern political values. Bayart (1980) stated that the Cameroon government condemned tribalism by passing a law on June 12, 1963, that prohibited any association from exhibiting tribal or clan behavior. Retired government officials remarked that the law also prohibited any clan objectives that contradicted national unity. The same law, which may still be in effect today and which discourages intertribal activities, is indeed a divide-and-rule tactic in that tribal groups cannot successfully plan strategies of improving their own environment without the government's permission, nor can they collectively oppose government laws. The government thus consolidates its power over other groups.

Some government members appoint people from their own tribal group to major positions in the cabinet rather than selecting individuals based on qualification. This colonial mentality impedes the growth of national consciousness in Cameroon. The campaign against tribalism practiced by such government members obstructs justice and stifles other opportunities for constructive criticism and opposition that could help negotiate around intercultural communication, integration and growth among most Cameroonians. The divide-and-rule approach fosters underdevelopment in Cameroon.

By adopting the colonial mentality, the postindependent Cameroon administration finds it even more necessary to perpetuate "colonial ideas" in Cameroon, for the following reasons:

• To keep interethnic rivalries under control, since over 200 cultural groups exist there
• To maintain a balance among cultural groups
• To ascertain the centralization of government authority. Total control and sectionalism seem to be common practices that slow development in any country. Some government members in Cameroon even resort to appointing their friends and family members to manage important decisionmaking positions within the administration (see Figure 3.2) . The administrative policy in Cameroon lends itself to failure and underdevelopment.

For any developing country to make policies regarding the rural areas, its government needs to consider individual opinions, normative values, philosophies, principles, and loyalties of its clanspeople or rural folk, since they constitute the majority of the nation's population. For social and administrative policies to be complete, they should be people-oriented.

Figure 3.2
The Typical Structure of Administrative Policy in Cameroon

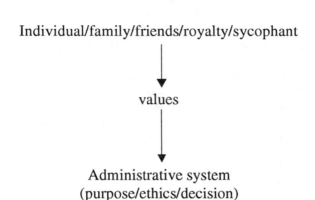

Individual/family/friends/royalty/sycophant

values

Administrative system
(purpose/ethics/decision)

Normative values of village society and individual opinions were channeled through clan meetings and/or the traditional ruler. Instead, the Cameroon government makes the laws and codes of ethics which become policies of the country's institutions. Policies should not be derived from friends, families, dynasties, and the political demagogues of the prevailing regime. Rather, the constitution should be based on the values and ideologies of rural residents because they constitute the majority of the population. The absence of the people's contribution to the nation's policy formation process shows that the society is controlled merely by individuals and interest groups. The policies so derived do not come from the people's dominant values but from eccentric individual postulates. Moreover, people in such communities believe that any ideology that negates a government philosophy is false, subversive, and deterrent to the national logos of peace, progress and unity.

The dominant ideology of Cameroonians is passive authoritarianism, publicly known as nationalism and politically described as communal liberalism. There is also a belief in Cameroon villages that no one can make a decision about an issue regarding the entire village other than the traditional ruler or his like. Thus, policies made by government officials are generally carried out in a docile manner, irrespective of their objective, goal, effect, or context.

Policies spread throughout the country as principles for the Cameroon people to abide by. The principles disseminated through the political party's literature and extensive campaigning by politicians and major government officials are considered societal values, for which all individuals are accountable. The main problem with this approach is that rural people, who are neither given the rationale behind policies nor allowed to exploit other options, simply believe what the politicians tell them and abide by the logos without reciprocating their thoughts. That one-way message-transmission procedure or bandwagon effect weakens communication between the villagers and the government and eventually slows change in the country as a whole. Such policies, and the procedures by which they are made, should be discouraged because the governments of such authoritarian systems do not last.

Finding the Right Policies for Cameroon's Development

The concerns just raised about policies are whether they should relate to all cultures within a society, given that over 200 ethnic groups exist in Cameroon. Since Cameroon is a multicultural society, the following imponderables arise:

- What makes a policy, and how is it adopted?
- Is it necessary that social, professional, and organizational policies determine the making of laws and social ethics?
- Do social, organizational, and professional policies necessarily become postulates of legal behavior?
- What values are considered when making policies? A strong administration should be able to address those issues (see Figure 3.3). Although this model shows communication as an incidental concern and does not account for lateral dealings with the various ethnic groups in Cameroon, it suggests a gradual breaking away from the authoritarian model, and it is arguably an appropriate step toward involving the Cameroonian people in major decisionmaking.

Figure 3.3
The Bureaucratic Model: Administrative Policy Process

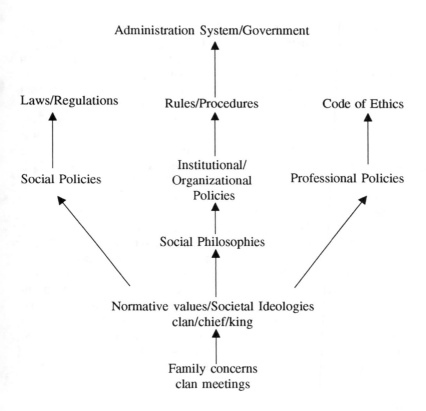

Practical democracy is a new phenomenon to the Cameroonian people, who have for hundreds of years been under authoritarian governance. People imposing their views on the central government would produce destruction, not a democratic climate for the enhancement of communication and development programs. History and experience show that any country that made drastic administrative changes had either civil wars or ruthless dictatorial governments that virtually destroyed free will and other democratic ideals. Such countries have normally faced serious socioeconomic problems.

Social and Economic Indices of Underdevelopment

Several development experts have called on development planners to be sensitive to the indigenous values of their target audiences. Interaction between the villagers and the government in Africa has been virtually nonexistent in an era of global change. African policymakers are psychologically and physically separated from their rural or peasant compatriots by such factors as education, geography and world view. Thus distanced, they tend to misunderstand the villagers' problems. This hinders their participation in group activities related to development.

The major social problems of Cameroon's rural communities include inadequate healthcare, nutrition, and information. Many villages lack health infrastructure. According to a study carried out by the Pan-African Institute for Development in Buea, Cameroon, very few health care centers existed; diseases like malaria and such symptoms as coughing and diarrhea increased. Patients had to be transferred to urban hospitals via bad roads (Pan-African Institute for Development, 1977, p. 3).

Those problems also haunt people in Cameroon villages, whose bad road conditions and long distances from hospitals cause them unease. The construction of a highway between two business regions in Cameroon's western province, Bafoussam and Foumban, on which about 60 trailers transport timber per day, was suspended by the African Development Bank because the Cameroon government failed to provide its own share of the funds. That slowed the transportation of farm-to-market products and other business transactions requiring the use of the road.

The Farmer's Cooperative Societies in Njinikom, Bali, and Tchubali, the northwestern regions, do not have a public relations department that can devise means to better monitor and extend their messages effectively to other farmers. That communication gap has led many rural and suburban dwellers to agitate against the present government, as reported in *Le Messager, The Herald, Cameroon Post*, and other local newspapers. This degree of social and economic neglect has a documented history. Zone study reports of the Fundong Subdivision (Kom) conducted in 1972 by the Pan African Institute for Development suggest a slow development of village projects. The reason for that slow change was that there were not enough communication techniques and/or media like radio, television, town criers, songs, and theaters to help disseminate information to the farmers. Even recommendations from the Fundong Subdivision Zone report (1972, p. 44) did not contain any information on the necessity of using the mass media to support the farmers' endeavors. The cooperative society in the Kom kingdom has not progressed much. Moreover, striving cooperative societies like "Mezam Meeting," which existed for more than 20 years, is losing its momentum (*The Herald*, January 3-5, 1994, p. 5).

There is, therefore, reason to assess the development needs of rural areas in Cameroon in general to determine the effectiveness of communications in supporting rural development. An assessment of rural Cameroonians' development needs requires a brief identification of the ethnic groups that make up the rural community.

Some Cultural Groups and Their Values

Cameroon is made up of people with diverse cultural practices (see Tables 3.1 and 3.2, which show the estimated strength and size of principal ethnic groups in Cameroon). Known as the "cultural crossroads" of Africa, Cameroon has over 256 ethnic groups in its land area of about 475,442 square kilometers. Certain groups can be identified by their group members, values, economic development activities, and interactive patterns.

The Bantu

The Bantu are made up of mainly Douala, Bassa, Bakweri, Batanga, Bakossi, and Mbo groups. According to Ardener (1956), the major economic activities of the Bantu since migrating to Cameroon have been fishing, agriculture, livestock, trade, "economic exchange" and crafts. The economic development of each tribe has been based on that tribe's ability to use manpower in exploiting its natural resources. Since the early 1920s, the Douala people have been building canoes out of wood for fishing (Ngwa, 1978). The Bantu interact in a cohesive manner by adhering to such values as property inheritance, exogamy, witchcraft and folklore.

Table 3.1
Principal ethnic groups: their distribution and estimated strength

Group	East Cameroun	British trust territory	Notes
I. Southern Nigerians		155,000	Ibo (25,800), Ekoi-Anyang-Boki, etc. Mainly now in W. Cam.
II. Northwestern and Coastal Bantu			Group with first European contacts. Ca. 70,000 now in W. Cam
Douala	45,000	2,000	
Bakwiri-Mboko		18,600	
Mbo (Bakundu)	25,000	44,410	
Bassa-Bakoko	195,000		
Other	2,000	4,000	
Total	267,000	69,010	
III. Equatorial Bantu			Beti-Pahouin includes: Ewondo 459,000 Bulu 128,000 Fang 48,000
Beti-Pahouin	655,000		
Maka	64,000		
Djem	41,000		
Other	13,000		
Total	773,000		

Table 3.1- *Continued*

Group	East Cameroun	British trust territory	Notes
IV. Pygmy	6,500		Mostly dispersed in isolated clusters.

Group	East Cameroun	British trust territory	Notes
V. Cameroon Highlanders			Bamiléké in E. Cam. living in départements of Dschang,
Bamiléké	549,000	51,800	Bafoussam, Mbouda, Bafang, and
Emigré Bamiléké	100,000		Banganté. Emigrés
Tikar and affiliates	12,500	260,000	live outside these five départements; ca.
Widekum and other Bamenda		114,000	427,800 of this group now in W. Cam.
Bamoun	80,000	2,000	
Banen	28,000		
Yambasa	26,721		
Total	796,221	427,800	

Group	East Cameroun	British trust territory	Notes
VI. Plateau Nigerians			In trust territory mainly hill pagans in Benué and south
Mambilla	12,500	36,000	Adamawa provinces. Ca. 30,000 of this
Tigon		15,000	group now in W. Cam.
Jukun		10,000	
Ndoro and Jibu		10,000	
Total		71,000	

Table 3.1- *Continued*

VII. Eastern Nigritic			Mostly pagans. Those in the E. Cam. often included as Kirdi. Ca. 20,000 of this group now in W. Cam. Chamba includes Bali.
(G)Baya	84,000		
Mbum	74,000		
Duru-Verre	43,000		
Vute (Bute)	17,000		
Namchi	16,000		
(T)Chamba	10,000	30,000	
Other	4,000	20,000	
Total	248,000	50,000	

VIII. Kirdi (northern pagans) Approx. total	450,000	367,000	Mostly pagan groups north of Benué River. In Brit. trust territory, mainly in N. Cam.
Prin. groups:		Prin. groups:	
Masa	80,000	Fali	
Tupuri	62,000	Koma	
Matakam	60,000	Bata	
Musgum	35,000	Highi	
Mofu	35,000	Marghi	
Gisiga	25,000	Njai	
Fali	25,000	Sukur	
Kapsiki	20,000	Bude	
Daba	18,000		
Mundang	15,000		

Table 3.1- *Continued*

IX. Islamized pagans			
Mandara	40,000	50,000	
Kotoko	25,000		
Total	65,000		

X. Chadic Shuwa (Choa)			Islamized Negroes of the Saharan fringe. Approx. 15,000 of this group now in W. Cam.
Arabs	45,000	52,300	
Kanuri	5,000	131,000	
Hausa	5,000	12,800	
Total	55,000	196,100	

XI. Fulani (Peul, Fulbe, Foulah, etc.)	395,000	72,400	Approx. 15,000 Fulanis now in W. Cam.

XII. Other			Mainly in South. Mostly Europeans and Americans, but includes Levantines, etc.
Non-Cameroons (Africans)	80,000	101,000	
Nonindigenous	16,400	1,142	

Composite grand totals	3,164,121	1,560,452	The 1963 U.N. Demographic Yearbook estimates total population of Cameroun Federal Republic at midyear 1962 at 4,326,000.
Latest official estimates of total populations	3,223,517 in 1959; 3,300,000 in 1961	1,632,000 in 1959; 1,586,000 in 1958	

Source: Le Vine V. (1964). *The Cameroons: From Mandate to Independence.* pp. 12-14.

Table 3.2

Estimated size of major ethnic groups in Cameroon

Ethnic Group	Number of Persons (in Thousands)
Northern Peoples (1)	
Fulani	400.0
Matakam	116.0
Massa	79.0
Toubouri	70.0
Fali	53.0
Baya	45.0
Guiziga	45.0
Moufou	42.0
Arabs	41.0
Guidar	38.0
Mousgoum	36.0
Moundang	31.0
Daba	28.0
Dourou	27.0
Kapsiki (and related peoples)	25.0
Kotoko	23.0
Mandara	17.0
Mboum	13.0

Table 3.2 - *Continued*

Western Highlanders (2)	Number of Persons (in Thousands)
Bamiléké	701
Tikar (and related peoples)	260.0
Widekum (and related peoples)	114.0
Bamoun	82.0

Southern Forest Peoples (3)	
Pahouin	705.0
Baloundou-Mbo	110.0
Bassa	95.0
Douala	60.0
Kpe	39.0
Baboute	17.0
Pygmies	6.5

Foreigners (4)	
Africans	50.0
Europeans (including Americans)	15.9

Code:
1 = Demographic survey for the 1960-61 period
2 = Demographic survey for the 1964-66 period
3 = Demographic survey for the 1962-64 period
4 = Mid-1960s estimate

(Source: Nelson, H. et al. (1974) *Area Handbook of the Republic of Cameroon.*

The Bantoid or Semi-Bantu

Known to be part of the Sudanic kingdom, the Bantoid or Northeastern Bantu occupy the central and eastern plateau in Cameroon. They are mostly situated in the Bamenda region which includes Babanki and Kom. The Bantoid produce coffee for cash and grow maize, groundnuts, cassava, yams, and beans for subsistence. Those people have a communal lifestyle. The male village residents build houses and do pottery and handicraft work, while the women fish, and plant crops. Some tribes manufacture and export such products as raffia bags, textiles, and woodcraft to other villages and import palmoil.

The Hemetic People

The Hemetic or Fulani (Peul) people live in northern Cameroon. They are a pastoral people whose chief economic activity is cattle-rearing. There are two kinds of Fulani: the Town Fulani who settle in groups and the Cattle Fulani or Borroro who search for green pasture to graze their cattle. The latter group has an independent lifestyle and adheres to religious beliefs.

The nomadic lifestyle of the Cattle Fulani has influenced their world view. They construct temporal homes using tree branches and grass and migrate to different parts of the country with their cattle to find green pastures. Their unsettled lifestyle makes it difficult for the government to carry out infrastructural development projects and to gather and spread information for their benefit.

The Bamoun

Also known as Bamoums, these Semi-Bantu who live in the east and Northeast of the Bamiléké region settled in Cameroon around the eighteenth century. The Bamoun people, whose lifestyle is very similar to that of the Northwestern Bantu in the Bamenda region, are said to be deeply involved in Islam, despite the introduction of Christianity in their community around 1906. King Njoya the reigning ruler at the time destroyed the church and encouraged Islamism among his people (p. 116).

The Bamoun still produce canoes, dance masks, sculpture, embroidery, bead and leather work. They have been known for building canoes from bamboos and timber to transport people and cash crops from farms to markets. The semi-Bantu remain leading designers of men's clothes and bracelets in Cameroon today.

The Bamiléké

There is no evidence of the origins of the Bamiléké. Ngwa (1978) has said that they might be part of the Tikars. The key geographical features of the Bamiléké landscape are savannah and forest. They rank among the highest producers of corn, kolanuts and coffee in Cameroon and are considered to be mostly commercially-oriented, in that they trade in goods from both within and outside Cameroon, and own most of the business units in Cameroon.

The Widekum

Emigrants from the Congo about 270 years ago, the Widekum people have a strong cultural variable — myth. Their main occupation is hunting, palmwine and palmoil production and poultry-raising. These people farm for subsistence more than for commercial agriculture. Like most Bantoid, their major communication channels are drums, horns and flutes.

The Kom (Bikom)

Known as Nkom, Bikom, or Bamekom, Kom is a kingdom with about 280 square miles and about 100,000 people. It has many mountains and rivers. It also has rich, fertile valleys in which most of the inhabitants live. Kom people are known in the northwest province of Cameroon for the production of masks, furniture, farm tools and utensils since the nineteenth century.

Big Babanki

Nkwi (1976) has documented that Big Babanki, also known as Kijem, Kidzem, Kidzom, or Finge was a part of Kom until the Germans separated the two kingdoms in the late part of the nineteenth century (p. 108). Big Babanki and Kom people share similar sociocultural and political practices.

The villages, for example, are presided over by a villagehead and a council of elders considered intelligent and influential. These individuals address issues confronting the village people. Kwifoyn, the most powerful authority, is at the head of the administration in the Kom and Kijem tribal communities. Administration, culture, economy, and communications among the Kom and Babanki people are more broadly described below.

Culture and Communication in Kom and Big Babanki

Interaction among the Kom and Babanki, people revolves around their belief in cosmology. American journalist, Fred Ferretti summarizes the general atmosphere in Kom during the absence of their deity Afo-A-Kom:

> It is not strange that there was a true sense of national loss, a crumbling of community identification, and a perceptible erosion of the Fon's power when the Afo-A-Kom was stolen from its royal sanctuary high in Laikom in the summer of 1966 (Ferretti, 1975, p. 7).

This deity was restored in 1973 through arrangements between a Cameroonian anthropologist and the American government.

Afo-A-Kom

Afo-A-Kom, better known by Kom people as Mbang, has a religious, political, economic, and communicative significance to the Kom people. An indispensable symbol of the history, beliefs, customs, and traditions of those natives, Afo-A-Kom remains a statue of royal importance to the Kom people. Ferretti (1975) acknowledges the potency of the statue and his understanding of and adherence to Kom tradition.

Kwifon (kwifoyn)

Kwifon is a society endowed with spiritual power and supreme authority in the village. According to a document published by Prescraft in Switzerland, 1993, Kwifon consists of "senior members who are executives of the traditional government, according to a Swiss missionary publication of the Kijem (Big Babanki) royal family tradition". The report also states that Kwifon functions are limited to protecting the village and conducting rituals on soil and population fertility. Kwifon also has the power to execute criminals.

One major political problem in Kom is the Christian church. The church seems to have created conflict among Kom people who live in the three great valley regions of the kingdom: Belo, Njinikom and Fundong. Akpey (1978) complains that Roman Catholics and Baptists in the kingdom, compete for church hierarchy. Some Christians believe that their denomination worships God better than other denomination. Such competition breeds distrust and dissension between the Kom indigenes and creates obstacles in the interaction and expansion of communication in the kingdom.

Indigenous Agents of Communication

Tradition has been handed down to Kom and Kijem people by word of mouth; myth, proverb, legend, song, invocation, folktale, incantation and riddle. Such creative forms of communication, which existed long before the written word and are still being used in certain remote parts of Cameroon today, serve socialization, didactic, and communicative functions in that they introduce the kingdom's generations to its values, customs, philosophies and beliefs.

Folktales

Folktales are highly functional in the village because they involve narrator-audience participation. Rules and norms govern the narrator's and listener's attitudes. The narrator has an eclectic mind. He often punctuates the story with names, places, and songs and enacts certain parts. The narrator begins with a question: "mun-ngana?" (May I tell a story?) and the audience replies, "Sun-ngain." (You may).

The narrator is often an older person thought to have the wisdom of the ancestors. That narrator often blends the story with lyrics and gestures to alert, persuade, or influence the listeners, who respond by providing a refrain in unison.

Here, the traditional rhetor not only helps bridge the knowledge gap between his or her audience and their ancestry, but also educates them with speech skills. Audience members can make use of those speech skills to provide rural development messages for their fellow compatriots if properly instructed by Africentric development experts.

The Extended Family

The Bantu or Tikars see life from a holistic perspective. Problems and triumphs are lavishly shared among other family members. In a population of over 100,000 Kom people, about 3,000 are educated in the Eurocentric tradition. However, the core of the Kom people's cultural continuity is the undestroyed family nucleus. Members of the broad family base observe kinship and other traditional customs of the family like funeral rites, and birth celebrations.

The family can be thus viewed as an institution that fosters social cohesion. The family is an environment whose members learn how to fit into society through mimesis. That school could use its cohesive ability to circulate health-awareness messages from experts and extend or spread them to other families. Phatic communion is a form of security for the less privileged members of the community, since through such communal activity the Fon or Bonteh and the common person come together. The genial atmosphere in which village people operate is conducive for gathering their perceptions and opinions concerning the mass media.

The Marketplace

Another typical environment in which heavy communal activity takes place is the market. In some parts of Cameroon, there are daily village markets, with the major market day occurring once every week. The tribespeople go there mainly to share information from one society to another. The market site is a milieu where information can be distributed. Many issues, persons and village events are discussed in the marketplace more than elsewhere. The market site could be used to disseminate rural development messages fast and effectively since most villagers go there. The information the villagers receive in the market should sensitize them to become more aware of their environment and to change it to suit their needs. That judgment is based on the assumption that "pictorial literacy develops proportionately with the amount of pictorial stimulation the individual is exposed to in his environment" (Fuglesang, 1978, p. 63). In addition to those factors, tribal values also play an important role in the sensitization process in that the individual bases whatever information he or she receives or perceives on his or her previous experience.

A study of Cameroonians' perceptions of the African concept of obedience toward the older person shows that there has been a rapid change in ethnic differences on values (Nwabuzor, 1980, pp. 214 -217). On the question of independent thinking in Nwabuzor's study, the Tikars, of whom the Kom and Big Babanki are part, were found to be unlikely to disrespect elderly persons. The study reported that five ethnic groups believed that teaching a child should be the parent's first priority. Other groups, like the Hausa-Fulbe, did not consider this value as first priority. From that study, one can deduce that group members of that tribe are prepared to sacrifice some of their values and change some of their thought. Although the study revealed that the Tikars are said to be less likely to change their opinions on recommending independent thinking for their children, it is likely that the perception would change if a similar study were carried out in the 1990s.

News Sources

Primary news sources in the two communities are groups, public gatherings, village leaders and masquerades. Messages meant for all villagers originate from the village elders but are transmitted by masquerades (masked dancers) and town criers. Some of the masquerades, which have spiritual value in Kom, come from the local administrative headquarters in Laikom. The Kvabula in Kom, for instance, disseminates ritualistic messages during public gatherings. Other news sources include the Fon's palace, liquor bars, private homes, marketplaces, festivals and drums. Certain special messages are disseminated at the Fon's palace and through drums. Interaction from the news source to the news receiver is mainly face-to-face.

Physical contact between news-source and news receiver is effective in that it makes the news current. However, news disseminated through person-to-person contact increases chances for the message to be taken less seriously, since the news-receiver does not receive the message first hand. Rumor-mongering appears to be the fastest communication device. Since the African village milieu is a closely knit thing through which every one knows everyone else, messages circulate quickly among the villagers but lose their currency and originality as more people share them.

The cultural values of Cameroonians are as diverse and complicated as the country's political system. In order to evaluate their notions of change and their ability to improve their interactions via several development support agents, it is important to briefly examine the current status of the Cameroon administration.

The PostIndependent Political System

Government

Cameroon operates under a strong executive authority vested in the President. Based on a 1972 Constitution, the President, apart from governing both the party and the country, is empowered to appoint and fire members of the government, negotiate and amend treaties, pass sentences against defaulters of society's ethics, and lead the armed forces (Ministry of Information and Culture, 1983). He has powers over the National Assembly whose members come from the 42 divisions/10 provinces of the country. The government claims that members of Parliament in the National Assembly are appointed to office by an electoral process, but popular belief is that government officials seduce voters with money to pick candidates that it wants. The president also appoints a person of his choice to a decisionmaking position, through a "presidential decree."

The members of Parliament are expected to raise the concerns, opinions, values, and socioeconomic problems of their people for the National Assembly to review and act on. The frequent concerns of the citizens range from lack of proper health care and transportation facilities to insufficient educational and infrastructural amenities in their community.

Development in the regions is chiefly carried out under the auspices of the ministry of Territorial Administration and Plan with some political assistance from the Party, whose main role is to sensitize the people to abide by and appreciate whatever efforts government makes to "develop" their areas.

The Constitutional System

Constitutions, especially those that pertain to communication and cultural activities, are mostly verbal declarations by ministers, the President, and members of Parliament. There is of course a Cameroon constitution, which confers authority on decisionmaking institutions (Forje, 1981, p. 27). The value system in Cameroon is based on the distribution of power and levels of interaction among the elites (see Figures 6 and 7). However, there have been agitations from other political parties and their stalwarts for the government to redesign the constitution using the people's values and opinions. The Union for Change, an organization that comprises many opposition parties, made a written request to the ruling government to hold a national conference in order to change the constitution. Within that request was the notion that the powers of the president would be limited . The government rejected the proposal.

The Judicial System

Justice operates in conjunction with the National Party's values and ideologies. According to 1983-1985 Press Reports in the Ministry of Information and Culture, the Head of State appoints members of the Supreme Court and selects the judges of the High Court, which has power over civil and criminal matters. The judges and lawyers in those courts are trained mostly in the French and British legal systems. The judicial, provincial and divisional courts are presided over by government appointed magistrates who often pass biased and uninformed judgment on cases that properly require the expertise and knowledge of tribe leaders who understand the *modus operandi* of their fellow tribesfolk (see Figure 3.4).

Although local courts are created to look into problems of village people, most cases in the village are taken to the divisional courts or Court of First Instance, and consequently to the Supreme Court (see Figure 3.5). In some cases, unsolved matters at the Court of First Instance are taken directly to the Court of Appeals. The Court of First Instance is the most active division of the judiciary, so far as rural people are concerned. Quite often, cases are determined by police officers or *gendarmes* who often use physical force to bring calm to the village community. Rural litigants often go unsatisfied, and this creates tension and conflict between individuals and villages.

Figure 3.4
Government and party distribution of authority

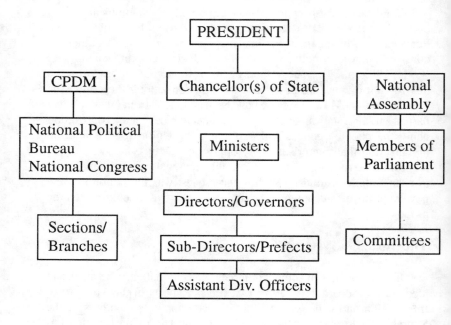

Figure 3.5
Structure of the judicial system

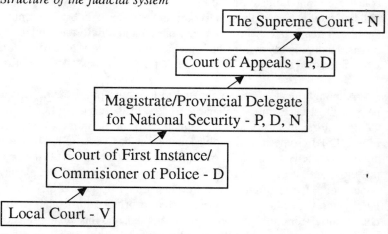

Code: N = National, P = Provincial, D = Divisional, V = Village

Land dispute, which is a big problem among rural people in Cameroon, is poorly handled by the court system. Apart from being unresolved by the courts, land dispute and corruption break down communication among individuals and tribes and between tribespeople and the entire government.

Current Administration

The country is divided into 10 provinces. Each province operates under the authority of a governor appointed by a presidential order. District and divisional officers perform administrative roles under the auspices of the governor. The district office, which acts as the lowest administrative unit of the republic, is supposed to facilitate any government-related activities for the district or village. The Divisional or district officer is endowed with the power to perform several duties. These include signing documents for village indigenes and using national code of ethics, laws, and regulations to settle problems related to private or individual property ownership, skirmishes, land disputes and other village inequities. The District Office transmits certain problems for the governor's action. The government's rationale for this procedure of administration is to "bring the administration closer to the people" (Cameroon in Brief, 1986, p. 26). It is meant to facilitate interaction between the public and the government. The system regulates the powers of the National Party so much that policymaking procedures and other national objectives involve the President. Thus, the communication pattern between the administration and the President is mainly one-sided — this is autocracy. The party and government are integrated machineries in the bureaucratic administration in Cameroon.

For any type of information from the Prefect to be considered for government action, it has to pass through several political channels. As such, it often takes months for decisions to be taken on issues that relate to rural development. Moreover, this political setup delays the projection and institution of rural projects (see Figure 3.6).

Figure 3.6
DecisionMakers and Distribution of Provincial Authority

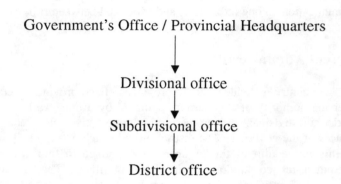

The CPDM preaches its political doctrine of democratization, rigor and moralization to rural people in a dictatorial way. Since 1987, newspapers have labeled the government an authoritarian entity, headed by a president who kills and punishes those opposed to his principles. A report in *Our People* (January 12-20) quotes the Prime Minister as commanding the national producers of local palm oil to reduce their prices by three percent rejecting their proposal to the government to reduce the prices for the chemicals and other items used in producing the oil. The government has allegedly been buying off rural people to join the sub section wings of its party and has forced other to adhere to government regulations and party activities.

British and French Policies

The status and mental development of Cameroon as a geoethnic-cultural and political region have been systematically established since colonial rule. Policies established without considering the philosophies and customs of the cultural groups, or even consulting the traditional rulers, promoted Franco-British autocracy and weakened the power of the local authorities. That tradition, including Christianity, is implicit in the administrative policies, philosophy, and economic future of Cameroon.

A brief historical statement describing the nature and impact of Christianity on Cameroonians follows.

The Missionaries

Christianity in Cameroon was effective in terms of converting the indigenes. The strategies used to convert them began when the missionaries convinced the indigenes that worshiping stones, rivers and other natural forms made them inferior to Europeans. Such practices as polygamy, paying of a bride-price, child marriage, ancestral worship and witchcraft were considered inimical to Christian principles and therefore discouraged. With the support and collaboration of Western political leaders, who provided those indigenes with foreign medicine and clothes, the missionaries were able to preach the scriptures in the hinterlands.

Christianity has served as a bridge to the material enrichment of certain Cameroonians who hold major posts in the government. The negative impact of Christian education in the developmental psyche of Africans stems from the notion that Christians are more civilized than believers in traditional religion. In a sense, many Africans see certain aspects of their own cultural values as primitive or hypocritical if the values contradict the teachings of the Holy Bible.

The effects of Western civilization may have been reflected in the daily activities of the indigenes as time went on. A different kind of education began to gain ground in Cameroon villages (see Table 3.3). Dialogue between sexes was weaker than before the missionaries. For instance, those taught to read and write were mostly male youths. Although the missionaries created high institutions of learning like St. Joseph's College Sasse (Buea), College Jean d'Arc (Nkongsamba), Cameroon Protestant College (Bali), Saker Baptist College (Victoria or Limbe) etc., where young Cameroonians could acquire socioscientific skills, (these schools have produced a cream of scholars and professionals), they failed to build schools where Cameroonians could improve their occupational potentials. The literacy centers set up in the village locale by the missionaries which urged and even forced the youth to attend bible classes were in fact Eurocentric assimilation camps for the defenseless, docile natives. The effects of inculcating foreign spiritual values onto an innate existing belief system were also devastating to the indigenes in that these indigenes were not encouraged to communicate in their own language. Secondly, the rural community became divided as followers of the missionary doctrine gradually isolated themselves from the diehard ancestral worshippers. The missionaries and the Cameroon converts considered other Cameroonians culturally inferior because they adhered to practices that the scriptures and/or missionaries condemned. It, thus, became difficult to maintain a balanced practice of traditional values. Indigenous languages were later translated into English, French, Dutch and other European languages and provided an effective medium of instruction in the missionary centers and schools.

Table 3.3
Official school schedule by german imperial ordinances in 1910

First year	Hours Per Week
Reading and writing (German)	2 hrs.
Moral principles and behavior	2 hrs.
Simple arithmetic	2 hrs.
Total	6 hrs.

Second year	Hours Per Week
Reading and writing (German)	3 hrs.
Moral principles and behavior	2 hrs.
Simple arithmetic	3 hrs.
Total	8 hrs.

Third year	Hours Per Week
Elements of grammar, orthography (German)	4 hrs.
Natural history	2 hrs.
Arithmetic	3 hrs.
Geography	1 hr.
Total	10 hrs.

Table 3.3 - *Continued*

Fourth year	Hours Per Week
Reading, writing, explanation of selected pieces (German)	4 hrs.
Arithmetic	3 hrs.
History of the territory	1 hr.
Natural history	2 hrs.
Domestic skills	1 hr.
Total	10 hrs.

Fifth year	Hours Per Week
Exercises in grammar (German)	4 hrs.
Metric system	3 hrs.
History of the German Empire	1 hr.
Natural history	1 hr.
Domestic skills	1 hr.
Total	10 hrs.

Source: Costeodat, R. (1930). *le mandat français et la réorganization des territoires du cameroun.* pp. 118-119).

The spirit of divide-and-rule still had a powerful impact on the natives. Several women's missionary societies were formed, but such societies separated the women from their husbands, families and traditional practices. This discouraged interpersonal communication and intertribal friendliness. Those influences, most of which still exist in Cameroon today, make it difficult for rural Cameroonians to communicate and adhere to a monolithic culture.

The value system in Cameroon is very complex, as it constitutes a blend of German, French, and English behavior and that of the indigenous tribes. An understanding of the cultural history of Cameroon requires serious consideration of the following situational variables, already briefly discussed in this study:

- The precolonial history of Cameroon
- The sociocultural practices of the colonial masters and the impact of the practices on the indigenous culture
- The origins and cultural practices of the tribal groups (that is, their own languages and world views, and their responses to natural phenomena)

Chapter Summary

This chapter has described the geohistoricocultural and communication environment in which Cameroon rural communities operate. It has also described foreign influences on Cameroon and the psychosocial status of ethnic groups in Cameroon across time. This analysis sets the stage for an understanding of the communication and development experiences of its rural people.

The fourth chapter discusses communication theories that relate to development communications, especially the dependency theory, and analyzes neoimperial media of communication and their effects on Third World communities. Case studies of the effective use of broadcast and local media in supporting development in Third World societies are also described.

CHAPTER 4

COMMUNICATION AND DEVELOPMENT:
Toward a New Framework

This chapter reviews the historical, social, and cultural climate in which media institutions of communication operate in developing countries. It builds a case for a communication environment in which rural people have shaped or can shape and reshape their *modus operandi* for development. It also argues that the media might have an impact on the behavior of their rural audience in Africa.

This chapter assumes that foreign cultures, through their communications media, may have weakened the development and communication concepts of indigenous groups. To understand the ways in which this weakening process may have taken place within these groups, the chapter explicates some salient theoretical and operational concepts that relate communication to development. It provides case studies wherein different forms of communication were used to support rural change in some African villages. It further describes the communication forms, like television and radio, that can best support development in terms of reach and accessibility.

Development is best determined within the cultural context of a society. That is, the values, beliefs, opinions, and expectations of people in a society determine the rate of development of that society. Furthermore, development is a concept, a perspective held by an individual or a group of people. The development of a society can be affected by certain interactions among individuals and/or groups that generate better ways of functioning.

In order to understand how interpersonal behavior in some Third World rural communities was affected adversely by Western culture, a brief discussion of neoimperialist constructs in Third World media follows.

What Does the NWICO Mean to Africa?

The concept of giving everyone an opportunity to listen and be heard through an international communication network, as proposed by "global village" advocate McLuhan (1964), stimulates everyone to embrace it instinctively, since it suggests a peaceful, united world brought into being through information-sharing. An adjunct to the concept of the New World Information and Communication Order (NWICO) is this: political, economic, and social issues and practices should be uniform, if not known to all through the magic of an international communication network. How else? Mowlana sees NWICO as an old phenomenon in contemporary international relations. In his article published in the *Journal of International Affairs*, (1993a), Mowlana complains that

> the technologies and institutions of communication that have become
> so central to world politics and economics over the last couple of
> decades have fundamentally altered the nature and sources of power
> and influence, both domestically and internationally (p. 59).

That complaint is predicated upon the notion that the progenitors and advocates of the global information order are in search of new territory to claim. This new interest, created mainly by members of the Non-Aligned Movement and some intellectuals, suggests that their reason for using communication media is to seek, acquire and increase their economic resources, not to use the mass media to inform people in other countries. The MacBride Commission (1980), an international group for the study of communication problems, stated that the advocates for this new concept demanded an equal distribution of radio frequencies, a reduction of international postal rates for printed material, fewer restrictions on copyright laws, protection of unapproved direct broadcast of satellite messages, and a rejection of the use of media for commercial purposes. Some of the contentions were probably raised by Third World — especially African — delegates at the UN, who have neither the technology to compete with technologically advanced countries nor the funds to purchase it.

Although NWICO's primary quest may be for global development, peace, and justice, cultural hegemony is, so far, the dominant practice, and international development only an incidental concern.

Can there be a global development in the 21st century if all of the NWICO demands were met? Is there something more to globalizing communication and/or information? Mowlana (1993a, p. 63) argues that the real NWICO quest is for a new *cultural* order, which surpasses the idea of mere communication and information. This suggests a fear or at least a suspicion on the part of low-context cultures (countries with smaller populations whose limited technology would make them less able to transmit their values internationally) that they may be overpowered in the 21st century. For countries with Anglo-Saxon traditions, like America and Britain, extending their values to the Arab world and some Third World countries would not only enable them to control the latter but would also enable them to sell their values in exchange for smaller quantities of Africo-Arab values, since Anglo-Saxons and English-speaking people dominate the world numerically.

Although African and other developing countries will benefit from Western technology through the NWICO process, they may be deprived of their resources in the communications bank; there is no guarantee that industrialized nations will fulfill all demands for equal information access. Africans have been lured and cheated before. They have never been compensated for the millions of slaves brought to the New World and for the economies they built.

From a sociopolitical perspective, Africa's socioeconomic transformation is the product of the NWICO. The popular uprisings in eastern Europe, the public demonstrations for democratic reform in China, the dramatic end of communism in the Soviet Union and its dissolution into smaller states, the unfolding democratic process and the dramatic end of apartheid in South Africa, the crisis in Somalia, the US presidential races, all publicized around the world through television and satellite connections, demand a redefinition of international sociology, politics, communication, culture and development.

The state of international communication today differs fundamentally in substance and structure from that projected by NWICO advocates two decades ago, in that smaller nations are overfed with and even intoxicated by the heavy one-way flow of messages from Europe, home of the most advanced communication technology.

International development follows the concepts of those countries with communication technology, whereas development planners in developing countries remain vulnerable and unable to push their own values. Hence they are obligated to follow the development patterns of others. That influence and the one-way information flow are partially accountable for the political instability in Africa. African leaders impose foreign development ideals on their citizens, in order to catch up with the rest of the world, without considering four key factors:

- The sociopolitical and cultural psyche of their masses is non-European.
- The architects of global development have a different perspective on the process.
- The technology of the distributing countries is very advanced because it took them many centuries to develop both their technology and their dominant ideas of human behavior.

Thus, any abrupt change from fundamentally Africentric behavior to a Euro/Asiocentric world view will prove catastrophic, or at least difficult, for African policymakers and their fellow citizens.

By submitting their demands for a fair distribution of communication systems — a well-intentioned effort — African delegates at the UN failed to foresee cultural domination from other member countries. They might regret having made the demand that the mass media be considered for anything but commercial purposes. When American media companies like NBC, ABC, CBS, CNN, the Associated Press, and United Press International decide to place their satellite dishes in South Africa or Burundi or Rwanda and expose the war and violence in those places, rather than concentrating their coverage on peace and development initiatives taking place in Ghana, where President Rawlings has been demonstrating methods of self-sustaining living among his people, it becomes more necessary for advocates of the NWICO to reconsider the impact of, or latent rationale for, foisting a new world information and communication order on less technologically advanced societies.

In hindsight, if the African delegates had not requested an equitable share of the world's communication and economic resources at the UN, they would still not have served Africa's interest, because their counterparts would still have used their technology to influence developing nations, despite Article 2, Paragraph 7 of the UN Charter, which mandates noninterference in the internal affairs of other states. Influential UN members like the United States, Russia and England, with economic and military power, have a history of meddling in the internal affairs of other countries.

It is no surprise, then, that developed countries are benefiting from the NWICO process. International communication specialists Preston, Herman, and Schiller (1989) and Giffard (1989) recall that following the demands some NWICO officials, the United States and other Western nations agitated against the African delegates' demands, claiming that if met, they would threaten a free market economy and the ideals of unrestricted flow of information. Free World proponents — the United States and its European allies — have triumphed. Information designed, processed, and disseminated by Western media is consumed all over the world. It dominates the world views of Third World nationals and of Africans in particular.

NeoImperialist Media in the Third World

Influenced by foreign mass media, Third World countries have emulated Western culture without seriously contemplating the repercussions. Whether cultural paradigms are social (dress patterns, marriage customs, love and courtship techniques) or economic, (the importation of VCRs, TVs, and other technological media forms), Western culture, *a travers* Western media, is still having damaging effects on Third World development agendas.

Western media transplant and export societal values and norms, and Western nations use their affluence to impose their ideas on cultures in Third World countries. People's reactions to media messages reflect the way the messages are interpreted and disseminated and the thoughts and memories that are consequently activated. Thus, the nature and extent to which Third World people interpret messages in the media depend considerably on the content of the media.

As in other African countries, the message content of Cameroon broadcast media did not influence the Cameroon rural people's efforts toward rural development, since most of the messages were disseminated in French and English — languages that were not indigenous to the rural people.

Developing through communication requires action that enables the individual to adapt to new levels of interaction. This study ascertains the effectiveness of forms of communication and interaction in the conservation of the resources of rural people in Cameroon.

In order to ascertain the effectiveness of communication in rural development in Africa, it is important to follow this chronological sequence:

1. Analyze, *grosso modo*, the scope of development communications and assess the theory and concept of dependency.
2. Analyze the paradigms that constitute the relationship between communication and development.
3. Examine the forms of intercultural media penetration and the *modus operandi* of the mass media.
4. Assess the overall concept of media influence.

Based on the analyses and conclusion, media concepts will be deconstructed by making some recommendations for developing countries.

Analyzing Development Communications

Communication and development, better known as development communication or the "dominant paradigm," assumes that a society changes through the application of new and old communication technologies. Development communication has been defined from a Marxist perspective by several Western scholars. Rogers (1989), for instance, sees the term as the application of communication with the goal of furthering socioeconomic change (p. 67). The mass media have the power to disseminate development messages and to persuade people to improve their basic living standards. Rogers (1989) further asserts that development communication includes composites of intercultural and international interactions.

Mowlana (1986) sees it differently. He believes there is a distinction between idealistic and functional definitions of development and intercultural and international communication. The idealistic human approach to international and intercultural communication "has been guilty of aiding and abetting international tensions, if not intentionally, then at least by not promoting peaceful solutions and not conferring legitimacy on the peacemaker" (Mowlana, 1986, pp. 180-182).

Although international communication has grown through human interaction and technological activities with the 20th century's proliferation of international travel and contact through telephones, faxes, and other telecommunication systems, relations between people of different cultures have only deteriorated. Intercultural and international communication as a process has failed in its role of improving relations between countries having different cultural practices.

The lack of interest in introducing and utilizing intercultural and international communication concepts to understand dissimilar cultures and improve international relations suggests that they are not practical constituents of development communications.

Development agencies like UNESCO, UNICEF, UNDP, IMF, The World Bank, and the Canadian International Development Agency (CIDA) consider development communications to be the use of hardware and software technology to support and/or promote social and economic activities.

The underlying view that communications support socioeconomic activities depicts development as a prerequisite for human existence. Third World nations invest heavily in radio and television in particular, hoping that those media will contribute tremendously to national development by reaching remote areas of their territories and the illiterate masses or rural audiences. For instance, during the 1970s and 1980s, the government of Cameroon spent millions of francs (CFA) to install radio stations in certain areas in the country to facilitate the processing and dissemination of information to those areas. In the early 1980s, the government invested more millions of francs in building of a TV plant in the hope that TV would inform and educate the Cameroon population faster and more effectively than radio and other media. The projects ran into financial problems. In addition, there were not sufficient programs to broadcast. Most of the programs broadcast addressed issues that were not relevant to the concerns of the indigenous population. As such, Cameroon TV did not satisfy the social and economic needs of Cameroonians.

Developing countries like Cameroon should use their media to spread adequate development information. To understand how that can occur, it is necessary to know the background of development communication.

Background of Development Communication

The concept of communications content as a support for socioeconomic development began in the West over 70 years ago. In America, it may have been initiated around 1922 by Lipmann, who wrote about the impact of moving images to the human mind in *Public Opinion*. Studies made by Schramm (1983, p. 6-17) reveal that communication began to be considered a development paradigm in the 1930s with the ideas of four "pioneering" American social scientists:

Harold Lasswell, Paul Lazarsfeld, Carl Hovland, and Kurt Lewin. As political scientist, sociologist, and social psychologists, respectively, these scholars sought to change notions of individual and group behavior. Berelson and Gaudet (1948) saw audience psychology as a necessary factor in determining the meanings of social phenomena.

Self-awareness and the development of habits to acquaint oneself with another person's behavior change a person's perception of his or her environment. Before change can occur, there must be motivation. Uncertainty causes motivation and both lead to information-seeking behavior. People tend to depend on the mass media for information, whether or not such information has positive or adverse effects.

Earlier studies alluded to the concept that the mass media retard social change. Lazarsfeld, Berelson and Gaudet (1948) argued that the mass media fail to raise essential questions about the structure of society (p. 505). Other communicologists looked at the mass media as carriers of capitalist ideologies. For instance, Hall (1980) contended that the "mass media are the most important instruments of twentieth-century capitalism" and that their main function was "ideological hegemony because they provide the framework for perceiving reality" (pp. 128-138). Hall seems convinced that the media seek to institutionalize bourgeois values, norms, attitudes, cultures, and beliefs by manipulating people's consciousness. The media present images and world views that people perceive as important.

Lerner (1958) has stressed the ability for communications to disseminate messages that are important to change. In his forceful work *The Passing of Traditional Society: Modernizing the Middle East*, published in 1958, Lerner encourages the use of Western models of development and/or modernization for all societies (pp. 46-47). Another influential author who has explored Western-oriented economic theories of development specifies four stages in the development process. Rostow (1960) looks at traditional society, establishment of conditions for takeoff into self-sustained growth, the drive to maturity, and the age of high mass media consumption. Those stages are the same ones taken by Western industrialized countries to develop their environment.

The electronic media are particularly important agents for development because they inform Third World audiences living apart from each other. Other communicologists like Pool (1961) and Schramm (1964), in addition to supporting the importance of the mass media in development, have asserted that the mass media have commercial use. In the late 1960s and early 1970s, researchers began to realize that some communication models in use impeded rather than promoted development in Third World societies. These researchers criticized nearly all models imported from the developed countries, including the "dominant paradigm." They became concerned that imported media programs contained information pertaining to changing the physical environment rather than conscientizing people's views on health care, nutrition, and other essential practices. The researchers sought local solutions for the proper use of the media in development, as seen in Ugboajah's (1985) book and in conferences and reports like those of the MacBride Commission. Using Western communication technology indeed created more development problems for countries like Samoa and Nicaragua.

Beltran (1976) and Rogers (1978) criticized the receiver-oriented paradigms of message diffusion and stressed the need to assess the philosophy and context of diffused messages. In some situations, development messages were considered irrelevant, and their anticipated effects were demoralizing (Rogers,1976, 1978).

Exploitation through public cinemas, radio, and the introduction of television in developing nations was engineered by political leaders and businessmen. Such US researchers of the critical theory school as Schiller (1969) and Wells (1972) have criticized the media and development paradigms precisely for promoting capitalism. They directly criticized America's role in exporting media products and using the media to advertise its products to the Third World, examined the unidirectional flow of media products from developed to developing countries and questioned the role of imported media products, especially television programs, in development. America exported media products to some developing countries not only to influence the psychology of the citizens, but also to lay the groundwork for direct economic investment. This strategy culled from the Marshall Plan was, as Mowlana recently realized, "the basis for much of the economic aid flowing from developed to developing countries since the 1950s" (1993, p. 11).

The influence of Western imported broadcast models on Third World broadcast systems was studied by another group of researchers. Most Third World nations' broadcast systems are tailored in the traditions of the British, French or American broadcast systems or all three, as in Cameroon. The BBC model of a public service corporation was supported by license fees; the French Broadcasting System, mostly state-controlled, was sustained through government and often commercial financing.

The American system has operated largely through commercial financing and through libertarian and social responsibility ethics. This system has survived the test of time in America because free will and freedom of expression are American values. While capitalism can and does prevail in America, it cannot survive in societies where the state controls the media and where dictatorship reigns. Thus, there would be risks in inheriting such models.

The process of transplanting or inheriting Western culture into foreign countries may distort the value systems of the foreign countries. The concept that the ownership, structure, distribution, and content of the media in any country without reciprocation by the country so affected, or prior target-audience consent is nothing short of media imperialism.

Besides inheriting inappropriate "Western" models, Third World nations found other shortcomings in foreign media systems. These shortcomings, related to the system's rapport with developed nations, included media imperialism, which involved a unidirectional flow of media products from developed to the developing countries, investments by the corporations of developed countries in the Third World, and media models. Some imported models were modified considerably. For example, Cameroon radio and television (CRTV), and Ghanaian television are largely controlled by the government, but they often run some commercials. However, this modification is limited. Other models, sparingly emulated, include Soviet and Asian models. Thus, several diverging systems exist in Third World countries.

Third World media systems fit all the categories developed by Schramm, Siebert, and Peterson (1956) in their acclaimed work *Four Theories of the Press.* Their theories have provoked researchers to develop other theories of mass media. McQuail (1983), for instance, outlines the following media objectives:

- Media should accept and carry out positive development tasks in line with nationally established policy.
- Freedom of the media should be open to restriction according to (a) economic priorities and (b) development needs of society.
- Media should give priority in their content to the national culture and language.
- Media should give priority in news and information to links with other developing countries that are close geographically, culturally, or politically.

- Journalists and other media workers have responsibilities as well as freedoms in their information gathering and dissemination tasks.
- To achieve development ends, the state has a right to intervene in or restrict media operations, and devices of censorship, subsidy, and direct control can be justified.
- Individual citizens and minority groups have rights of access to media and rights to be served by media according to their own determination.
- The organization and content of media should not be subject to centralized political or state bureaucratic control (McQuail, 1983, pp. 95-97).

The common assumption underlying McQuail's list of objectives is that a government or parapublic institution should control the programming and dissemination of certain media messages. Policy recommendations following the new international information order critique reflect the stance that only governments can stand up to foreign pressure. The World Bank, Food and Agricultural Organization (FAO), UNESCO, and other international aid donors closely associated with Western economies do not support the argument that basic indigenous development incentives and objectives should be set by indigenous governments and that state-controlled agencies should be given priority in development projects.

Media tend to be seen as agencies for development, planned and operating according to state objectives. As Third World countries struggle with such international agencies and changing models, Third World countries should provide fertile ground for the application of numerous mass communication media. Those countries may need to use electronic media, especially TV and radio, to spread rural development messages more rapidly, widely and easily. To understand the latter position, this study probes into the connection between communicating and developing.

Relationship Between
Communication and Development

Schiller (1969) has identified some perspectives in the examination of the relationship between communication and development. One of the three approaches, the pluralistic approach, deals with the enumeration of substantive variables of ethnocentricity, and it relates mass media to different development constructs. The "missionary" or "philanthropy" paradigm advances the notion that an understanding of the fundamental relationship between developed and developing economics requires comprehending the role of the media. That paradigm studies the contribution of the media in promoting Eurocentric capitalist development. This latter view is economics-oriented, and it discusses the course of development within the scope of each nation (Gurevitch, Bennett and Woolacott, 1982).

The "philanthropy" approach is Marxist because it regards certain norms of complex or stratified industrial societies as composites for survival. That view, according to some theorists, strengthens the concept that industrialization could be facilitated in some societies if the norms were generated (Bologh, 1979). Such a functional perspective of the media has been supported by several communication and social science researchers. For instance, Sarti (1981), a communication scholar, has argued that the "mass media could contribute to the process of overcoming some of the problems of underdevelopment" (p. 317). The present study is predicated upon that position.

However, Sarti's view has been intensely challenged by Schiller (1976,) and Mattelart (1976) as loaded with ideologies of domination. The mass media expedite commercialization and industrialization in major economies and Western media create a pluralistic culture in monocultural communities. Pluralistic culture weakens the communal lifestyle that has existed in developing rural communities for a long time. Rural communities in Africa are held together by indigenous values and modes of interaction. Therefore, any introduction of foreign values through the media, trade or industrialization would distort the existing fabric of an indigenous culture and thereby weaken interaction among rural people. The present researcher is also concerned that foreign values disseminated through African TV stations may have had a negative influence on rural people, since these stations do not appear to have enough locally produced programs.

Foreign values are indeed disseminated through Third World media. However, such African heads of state as Ahmadou Ahidjo and Paul Biya and information ministers in Uganda, Nigeria, Kenya, Tanzania, and Zimbabwe see the mass media as national development agents. A discussion of communication and development from an African point of view follows.

Communication and Development: The African Experience

The influence of the media on African resources can be said to be so great that Western societies appear to satisfy their agricultural, educational, nutritional, and technological objectives at the expense of Third World planning and rural development schemes. In understanding the dialectics and effectiveness of Western media influence on African culture, general knowledge of the use of communication for development is important. Africentric scholars and mass communication policymakers need to understand:

- How communication operates in the process of behavioral change
- How to plan, produce, and evaluate the communication message in a particular field
- How community needs and attitudes can be researched through the mass media
- What media are appropriate and available. Policymakers should have accurate information that will be spread to the target audience through specific communication channels, popular to that audience and appropriate for them and for whatever projects will be carried out.
- The development communication model that discusses a shift from electronic media concepts to using other modes of mass communication in strategizing rural-based programs on agriculture, job creation, and health care.

These goals can be realized if a mediating group can effect an agreement on the purpose, objectives, methodology and content of the project to be developed and methods of message delivery and can get approval of target audience participation. A well-developed program can be very useful if the mediating force includes people from the area in which the project needs to be implemented.

Unfortunately, Western media do not observe the above procedures for development. In very few cases, only face-to-face interviews take place. Western countries send their representatives to meet officials of African countries to discuss ways of improving communication skills between them. For example, in 1987, journalists from about 15 African countries were invited to Washington, D.C., to discuss with American journalists how to better disseminate information through their national electronic media among their citizens. Apparently, one of the effects of such meetings is that the delegates are encouraged by their Western counterparts to use media equipment developed in Western countries. The delegates' countries may purchase that equipment in the hope that it would contribute to the development of their societies. Because such Western media equipment as radio sets, cameras and VCRs are portable and accessible to rural areas in developing countries; their messages are capable of influencing illiterate rural audiences.

Commercial electronic media and meetings between Third World news reporters and Western reporters can be agents of political control. They are products of political sycophancy in that the Third World reporters are advised to encourage their fellow citizens to purchase foreign goods through advertising in their national media, in the hope that the citizens would rapidly learn from using the goods and/or improve their ideological and behavioral standards. The result is that the trained media reporters and products change people's attitudes and behavior.

That perspective is also takes by Lerner (1958) in an examination of the theory of modernization. He stresses that media play a role in creating awareness in developing countries. Developing communities are placed in a precarious and vulnerable situation because their media disseminate information that contributes to a change in traditional customs.

Economist Rostow (1960) puts the theory of change into five categories:

1. small society,
2. establishing preconditions for procedure,
3. having a premise of self-sustained growth,
4. departing to maturity, and
5. reaching the stage of high mass media consumption (Rostow, 1960).

The concepts developed from Rostow's theory of development apply to the Third World, although they contradict the approach policymakers of African countries adopt. Rostow implies that a society needs to have specific objectives in order to abide by the rules that govern it. Then that society should establish some conditions for self-sufficiency. One of the preconditions for such self- sufficiency includes consuming mass media content as a society and, by so doing, relying on the reconditions for material growth.

The Anatomy of Dependency

Dependency is a theory coined by Latin American development scholars which defines the marginalization of Third World countries by developed ones. This theory looks at Marxism or the development of poor economies through the prism of Western philanthropy. Dependency is synonymous with underdevelopment. A dependent government does not develop its own incentives or make optimum use of its resources to improve the living standards of its people. Although research has been done on how changes in media institutions change social environments and what effects they may have on people's behavior (Meryowitz, 1985, p. 15), media planners in African countries do not seem to be putting enough effort into improving the quality of media equipment and programs because their governments dictate these to them.

The United States of America, Britain, Germany, France and other powers are guilty of media imperialism in that, as modern capitalist nations, they make developing countries depend on their lending. In exchange for their services, these capitalist powers impose their political policies on and even intervene in the governing procedures of the countries they help. Some writers have discussed the issue at great length, especially those who have experience in the mass media. Media analyst Cohen (1963) asserts that US media, especially the press, cover events in foreign countries in order to achieve specific US foreign policy objectives.

US media have not only historically played influential roles in reporting atrocities and events in Third World countries, or in countries with small economies, but have also used imagery to orchestrate results and impressions that reality and reason could not have obtained. In the case of the Persian Gulf War, the US media have been charged with conveying a sense of America's triumph to the American and international audience prior to the war's conclusion (Mowlana and Schiller, 1992, abstract). US media coverage eventually helped the US government to convince NATO allies and the UN Security Council to pressure Iraqi president Saddam Hussein to go to war. Reports from *Time Magazine* from August 1990 to December 1990, especially the December edition (pp. 25-38), *The Washington Post, New York Times, Chicago Tribune*, and powerful television networks with large international audiences like CNN, CBS, NBC and ABC, were relatively negative toward Iraq because the US and over 150 members of the United Nations objected to Iraq's occupation of Kuwait. CNN, for example, spent over 100 hours reporting on the war. Seventy-five percent of the coverage by other mainstream media in the US favored US involvement in the war by projecting Iraq as an aggressive country and its President as another Adolf Hitler. About eighty percent of the stories in the print and electronic media declared the US the victor, while the war was still being fought. Monroe (1991), editor of the *Washington Journalism Review* says the main aim of the US defense administration information process was to prevent the public from foreseeing a Vietnam-like catastrophe resulting from the US involvement in the Persian Gulf War. Williams (1990) of the *Washington Post* stated that the Pentagon was happy with its information tactics. Luostarinen (1991) says the US government "has every reason to be satisfied with the way the war's publicity was taken care of" (p. 13).

Although analysts (Malek and Leidig, 1991) contend that the press relied on the government's interpretation of the crisis in order to mobilize the American public to understand its objectives, the heavy coverage by American mass media and America's crackdown on Iraq had an overwhelming impact on international viewers with lesser media technology.

People in African countries, who fall into this latter category, may have been susceptible to US media influence during and since the war. Due to its relatively small audience and limited resources, the African press, including *Afrique Économie, Afrique Asie, West Africa, The Guardian* (Nigeria), *African Mirror, Al-Aram, New Vision* (Uganda), *Times* (Zambia), *Cameroon Tribune, Ghana Daily, The Standard, Nation* (Kenya), *New Vision* (Uganda), could not handle the coverage with the same intensity as the American press, or affect readers' views on the rationale for, and cause and effects of, the war. Inasmuch as the American press did not stimulate more debate and/or objective arguments on the Gulf Crisis, it suggested the extent to which dependency can affect the economy and people's world views and how governments can use powerful media outlets in their countries to control the opinions of others.

A high-ranking official in the US government used the American media to support America's role in the Somali crisis. Secretary General Warren Christopher, in an interview in *Time* (October 18, 1993), told the world that American troops would be used wherever the US had vital interests (p. 46). That statement was followed by a deployment of about 22,000 US troops to Somalia who, besides killing Somalis alleged to have caused the civil war there, offered them food and medical assistance. Some Muslim fundamentalists might have seen that philanthropic gesture as the luring of Muslims into Christianity, bearing in mind that Somalia is largely a Muslim country and America a Christian society. That the world saw pictures of young Somalis scrambling for bags of food being dropped by US soldiers on US TV networks (with their satellite plants around the world) suggests the broadcasters' intent to depict African socioeconomic and political helplessness.

All of the above-discussed issues of US media coverage of the livelihoods of low economies or countries with small economic infrastructures and culture nations that practice different religions and politics like Iraq indicate that US media have tremendous influence over certain activities and events in foreign countries. Other concepts of Western media interference in Third World cultures are assessed below.

Western Mediametrics and Third World Cultures

"Mediametrics" means the mathematical activity of electronic media. Foreign media, especially in Western societies, interfere considerably in the socioeconomic progress of Third World countries. That type of inteference raises the question of the media role in Third World countries. Culture analyst Hall (1977) argues that foreign customers tend to interfere and/or penetrate high context cultures through the media. Such penetration hampers the development of indigenous commercial media techniques. In other words, Third World media audiences are more likely to purchase foreign products than to purchase indigenous products advertised on their own media. The reason for this preference is that the audiences are familiar with the indigenous agencies advertising local products, while foreign products are somewhat "strange" and therefore demand more attention.

A country should control its own media because its economic powers are weak and its consumers' motivation needs different from those of the foreign countries. For instance, Cameroon, which has over 256 ethnic groups and languages and which imports several TV programs from

France, the US and Britain, broadcasts relatively few commercials from local companies. TV viewers in Cameroon seek to emulate the often rich and sophisticated lifestyle of the people they see in the imported programs — without the necessary amenities. Such US television dramas as "Dallas" and soap operas are seen on Cameroon television at least once a week. Although the main objective of the imported programs is to bolster America's social image, the latent economic effect on young Cameroonians could be severe. Young Cameroonians, including village inhabitants, may become more extravagant and spend more money on clothes, dinners, and parties than on economic investment.

If Western media have such personal interests in Third World countries, how are Third World traditions to be protected? How do concerned intellectuals, developers, and governments of developing countries save developing countries from losing their social and economic power?

Third World governments should perpetuate indigenous ideals and values and develop media agendas that blend electronic and traditional messages in order to retain indigenous values and generate change among Third World peoples. Makinde (1986) and Nwanko and M'Bayo (1989) stress that African mass communication researchers should look at African conventions in their deliberations on mass communication. That request is crucial to the social economic advancement of Africa because there is limited communication for development. Illiteracy is so common in rural communities that print information outlets like newspapers would not serve the rural people. Moreover, the readership of that communication medium is limited to urban residents (Awa, 1988, p. 131). Another crucial issue is that Western modes of communication like radio, video and TV do not merely function as homogeneous links in heterogeneous cultures but also depict a certain image to the diverse and gullible Third World audiences.

Two scholars of mass culture and media effects maintain that media induce changes in human attitudes and cognitions without respect to human cultural values/environment. Viewers allude to the fact that viewers or audience members consume media content without interpreting the messages or giving feedback. This inability to reciprocate information (Chaffee and Hochheimer, 1985) is responsible for the slow response to development programs put forward by most government media in developing countries. The media planners in those countries do not seem to design and disseminate programs that promote indigenous culture. However, research has been carried out by some Third World planners to monitor Western media programs in their own countries. It suggests that there are alternatives. There are instances where some countries successfully reduced the proportion of imported electronic appliances.

Before finding a solution to the problem of media imperialism, Third World countries need to create their own communication policies. Simple as it may sound, subtle imported cultural concepts can be reformed by any government determined to change and/or establish its own agenda for development. The agenda should have minimal foreign influence. While these concepts are highly debatable, in that governments of new nation-states depend on media programs that promote an integrative culture, such concepts can be used to improve media programs and to promote indigenous cultural paradigms. Even when seeking assistance from foreign governments, the governments of new nations should ensure that such assistance is compatible with crucial development objectives. The former president of Zambia has asked Westerners to examine the history of Africa in order to understand the instability and socioeconomic needs of African nations. In an interview on *The Hilltop*, Kenneth Kaunda asked Western powers to offer assistance only as a supplement to fair methods of trade (1994, p. A2).

Developing nations try to predict the future in order to stabilize their sociopolitico-economic potential. Herbert (1981) asserts that "predictability and stability must be modified by the human desires for autonomy, challenge, and competence" (p. 467). According to Herbert (1981), group organization is necessary to cause development.

Group consciousness can expedite development in Third World countries. To develop indigenous group consciousness, Third World people should promote their own culture through the media. These countries can reduce Western media influence by promoting the use of traditional or local modes of communication in the rural areas first because rural residents constitute the majority of the population and they still use much traditional African culture. The governments, in collaboration with traditional rulers, need to style their information systems to correspond with such indigenous modes of communication as village gatherings, town criers, drums, and flutes. These media are affordable and have no spatial or temporal limitations on the number of users. They are also gratifying, in that the languages used to transmit messages are indigenous, familiar, and comprehensible to the users, as Makinde (1986), Riley (1990, pp. 301, 304, 306) and other development communication researchers have said.

In addition, Western media are expensive, especially to nations that have television plants, like Nigeria, Cameroon, Ghana, and the Ivory Coast. If these nations reduce the number of programs imported and promote a national interest in local programs, the "home-brewed" programs would help alleviate local negative cultural constructs cause sickness, death, and poverty and worsen people's living conditions.

In many developing countries, there are relatively small markets that sell commodities from major foreign advertisers. Third World countries' ability to purchase mass media products from foreign countries is low, however, compared to that of developed countries. Western media development of marketing conditions, political overpowering, and linguistic acculturation of developing countries would not prevail if Third World countries purchased fewer goods imported as a result of foreign media programming.

In order to overcome those obstacles to development, developing countries must understand their milieu, depend on that milieu, and act meaningfully and effectively within the original cultural context of that milieu. Effective action here refers to the ability to tackle such quotidian problems as financial self-development and alienation from fellow citizens who speak unfamiliar languages and practice unfamiliar cultures. Developing countries should become more socialistic and should practice what this researcher calls rural utilitarian communism. This is the process whereby rural people in countries with poor economies improve their skills, creativity, knowledge-sharing incentives, and farming and carry out more physical and intellectual activities among themselves. They should also be willing to destroy those cultural taboos that increase disease, poor health and poverty.

The greater the need for collective and effective action and the stronger the autonomy of Third World citizens, the less the chances that messages supplied by the Western media will alter behavioral and cognitive patterns in the Third World. Promoting indigenous programs for the enlightenment of the masses requires extensive use of modern and traditional forms of communication. As stated earlier, local media are cheaper and more available to the poor than imported high-technology media. An argument for limiting the use of electronic media and promoting the use of local media is provided in the next section of this study.

Communication Technology in Development

Development scholars have been concerned about the use of communication technology in elevating the social and economic standards of developing countries in order to cope with the modern standards of the West. The objectives for using hardware and software technology to meet the needs of rural sectors in developing nations have been emphasized in recent years. Hardware technology, computers, light and heavy machines, and other equipment that facilitate production is imported to and heavily consumed by developing countries. In addition to the numerous tractors that tear down the forests and the many foreign companies that construct roads linking villages, most policymakers in developing countries continue to import hardware technology to industrialize and "civilize" their country.

The leaders of those countries believe in using hardware to change the physical structure of their environment. To enhance the physical evolution of the environment, some governments encourage the use of such software technology as radio, TV, video, audio recordings, and visual aids whose informational content is basically Western/foreign. Whether rural populations appreciate the importation and use of hardware and software technologies in their environment or not, those technologies support the changing of agricultural practices, literacy, transportation, and other aspects of rural people's daily lives. According to a 1976 report released by the Program of Advanced Studies in Institution Building and Technical Assistance Methodology at Indiana University, "appropriate technology" is necessary for the improvement of local conditions. The report states that appropriate technology is the "direct link connecting needs to organized and rationalized means of satisfying those needs. Appropriate technology considers the local, natural, and human resources and encourages indigenous initiation and innovation" (1976, p. 4).

Appropriate technology means that local inhabitants participate in the determination of objectives for the local environment. In order to set those objectives, individuals in a particular environment need a structured educational program.

Learning from experience is effective in developing countries, given that the mass audiences who make up the rural population do not have physical and financial access to educational institutions with structured programs.   In order to teach these audiences, it is necessary to use structured and more informative rural-oriented programs. Such programs and innovative multimedia forms of communication can energize, motivate and consequently lifestyles of rural people. For Kulakow (1984), telephone systems, folk media, graphics, popular theatre and satellite communications are also helpful in assisting development (Kulakow, 1984, p. 2). Kulakow demands that radio and TV be "publicly exhorted to produce more programs focused on development projects" (1984, p. 3). That overall view of the broadcast media is synthesized in the MacBride Report, the International Commission for the Study of Communications.

The MacBride Report points out that

> communication should be seen as a major resource, a vehicle to ensure real political participation in decisionmaking, a central information base for defining policy options, and an instrument for creating awareness of national priorities (1979, p. 488).

This study discusses the effectiveness of TV, radio, and traditional media in rural development in Africa. While the study does not disregard the potential for or effectiveness of other media of communication in supporting development, the present researcher assumes that the communication agents selected for the study — TV, radio, and traditional media — will help suggest effective ways of interacting within rural communities for development purposes.

An Analysis of Pedagogical Television (PTV)

According to propaganda scholars, television has an educational function, in that it stimulates viewer response. Other scholars also share the same view but point out that a developer's theoretical and ethical values should influence the degree to which television messages change the society.

In order to analyze the importance of using TV for the development of rural areas in Africa, it is necessary to briefly discuss some of its functions, review aspects of pedagogical TV, and examine the arguments advanced by certain authorities on the TV industry. The primary function of TV in Africa is to increase awareness among the people and to assist the masses (the rural people) in their development endeavors. Apart from providing moving pictures of villains and saints, TV teaches viewers how to conform to or deviate from certain social ethics. Some theorists have noted that TV contributes to or affects the psychological development of its viewers (Ball, Palmer and Millward, 1986, p. 130). TV is thus designed to control the society and make profit from controlling it. That Marxist concept shows a conflict between the "object" (the culture industry) and the "subject" (the consumer or audience). It also depicts repressed subjectivity.

However, television messages tend to flow only one way, from the TV agenda-setters to the vulnerable audience, and not vice versa. Bologh (1979) has argued that one form of life may reproduce itself one-sidedly as a compulsion in which active desiring controls the subject (p. 7). As divided subjects or ethnic groups, the Cameroon rural people, for instance, may become so obsessed with the moving pictures on the TV set or fascinated by the magic of TV that they cannot conceptualize or interpret fully its ideological content.

The underlying concept here is that persons who watch TV tend to digest its content, since they have no control over its broadcasting, especially persons in societies where TV is a new phenomenon. In countries like El Salvador, Samoa, Cameroon, and Niger, scholarship through TV has not only de-educated the populace, but also has to a great extent persuaded people to favor foreign cultural constructs over their own. In other words, the form and content of TV programs in these countries are nonindigenous, and the effect is that indigenous citizens become acculturated or educated in a foreign culture without fully assimilating their own culture.

Given the above *lusus naturae*, one may posit that there are social and political implications of pedagogic television (PTV) in developing countries that need to be addressed. It is important to discuss the role and nature of TV scholarship in the maintenance, integration, and transformation of these nation-states. In looking at the situation, the following questions arise:

- Which groups in these countries would benefit from PTV programs?
- Whose values are to be transmitted and in whose language?
- Who should determine the content of the programs?

- What skills should be developed, by which group, and for what purposes?
- How effective and extensive would the PTV programs be?
- How effective would be the group's level of participation in the programs, and what role would the participant play in the decisionmaking process for the individual or group?
- Does the scholarship acquired through viewing TV reflect the true lifestyle of the rural residents?

In order to examine the above questions, it is necessary to look at the role and nature of PTV in the so-called Third World countries. The next section of this study describes the sociopolitical implications of PTV in developing countries and recommends certain criteria for educating people in the developing countries, including Cameroon.

Review of Scholarship and Pedagogical Television

Since the reconstruction period in the West, TV scholarship has been considered the key to modernization. Some new nation-states in the developing world have been struggling to overcome conditions of underdevelopment by scholarship to:

- Transmit common values and develop a national identity and consensus among diverse, often brawling, tribes
- Train and select the technicians, professionals, and leaders required to manage complex economic and political institutions
- Develop skills in the population at large so that they can participate in the nation-building process.

The mass media cannot bring about a miracle in educational systems. Any technology that enables a country to expand and improve its scholarship is an instrument for change. Such technology can be used to overcome unequal opportunities, integrate previously excluded people, contribute in the development of individuals and their social groups, and help achieve widespread consensus and solidarity in a heterogeneous society. PTV programs can also favor advantaged groups, establish barriers to collective development efforts, and deprive people of their individual and collective identities.

Unless a country deliberately and systematically pursues a well-defined policy to achieve equality in educational opportunities, achievements, and wealth, the likelihood of past socioeconomic inequities prevailing would be would be great. On the whole, however, underdeveloped countries do not usually pursue policies regarding equality in education and achievement. They tend to deal mostly with political crisis.

PTV messages have not been reaching the most disadvantaged populace in underdeveloped countries — the rural poor. Where programs were directed at disadvantaged populations, their content was often inappropriate and produced poor results, because such content represented values typical of dominant groups in society. An examination of showcase countries for educational television, such as El Salvador, Samoa, Cameroon, Niger, and Mauritania, reveals specific perspectives.

In El Salvador, TV was initiated at the junior high school level (Speagle 1972). In Samoa, PTV was used to achieve universal primary and secondary schooling.

Perhaps the most imaginative utilization of TV took place in Niger. Plans to expand the project with French assistance were constrained by the poverty of the Niger government and by government plans to delimit education to less than 50 percent of the relevant school-age population.

In Cameroon, a country with over 11 million people (Ministry of Planning and Territorial Administration, 1985, p. 15), instructional programs such as "Our Changing Agriculture" and Congress meetings have been broadcast in English and French. Only about 35 percent of Cameroon's population understand these languages. Most of the speakers of the two languages live in the cities or urban areas. The effect is that very few Cameroonians — the well-to-do — get more education and training to better their own conditions and scarcely help improve their country's development objectives, while the masses remain in ignorance and poverty.

The likelihood of getting most Cameroonians involved in their own linguistic development is small, in that over 256 languages are spoken in Cameroon. It becomes even more difficult for them to abandon their own language and its cultural connotations to receive instructions in a foreign language. Moreover, most Cameroonians think differently in their varied languages, and that makes it difficult for them to substitute their culture for English and French cultures. The question of whose values need to be reflected in the curricula is complex and volatile in newly independent nations. Tribal and linguistic groups that have little in common with the entire nation may not learn anything from TV when they consider the TV set and its "magic" as strange and foreign. Thus, using PTV to achieve consensus and development in Cameroon would hardly be successful.

The extension of scholarship through TV to disadvantaged rural children and underemployed and unskilled adults, for instance, raises the issue of what programs are to be transmitted. In the case of rural education, TV may be seen theoretically to present the rural masses with an ideal opportunity to understand how to develop common skills, messages, and experiences among all people. TV must provide rural people with the opportunity to transmit the particular skills and knowledge that enable them to cope successfully with their own milieu and attain a decent standard of living.

Using schools and the media in Cameroon to integrate village individuals into a holistic, hegemonic cultural fabric by undermining local and parochial cultural constructs, or completely excluding any allusion to them from the TV curriculum, may have an adverse effect on the village audience. Any threat to the social and cultural identity of rural individuals represents a threat to their self-identity and well-being.

In some societies, members of the minority or nondominant social groups have not been vigorously engaged in the scheduling or development of educational programs. In many cases, members of the urban elite collaborate with excolonial superpower nations to plan and develop media agenda for the rural people. The programs are mostly sponsored by such international bodies as UNDP, IMF, the World Bank, USIA, UNESCO, UDEAC, UNICEF, even the Peace Corps.

The dominance of urban groups and external donor countries is seen in the decisions made about which language should be used as the medium of instruction and for the setting of national codes of ethics. In several multilingual societies, TV is used to teach a common language within the country. TV is then used to communicate with the outside world. In most African countries, the language of the excolonial master or trust power is English and/or French. A strong case might be made for using an international language as the medium for instruction because there are many native languages spoken in most African societies. Countries like Cameroon and the Ivory Coast, where no indigenous language group seems to dominate may opt for French.

As already mentioned in this study, Cameroon has 256 spoken languages. Selecting one indigenous language in which to broadcast messages would mean favoring one ethnic group over the others, and that would undoubtedly precipitate tremendous hostility among ethnic groups within the country.

To what extent is cultural synchronization feasible in African societies that are basically multiethnic, with many language codes and rituals striving to preserve their norms, histories, philosophies and basic rules for human conduct? A tentative answer is that Third World culture should be pluralistic. Some Eurocentric values should no longer dominate information dissemination techniques and development concepts in the African continent. There should be a process of maintaining peaceful multicultural coexistence. Blake (1993) calls for a revolution in communication techniques. In his article *La fin des visions eurocentriques,* he argues that in order to improve the standards of their people for the 21st century, African policymakers and development planners should avoid using technical development problems culled from European values. One problem may be the heavy use of European languages in the African press.

The issue of choosing a language for PTV purposes must be decided by Africans according to their own development objectives. There are ways in which developing countries can adopt a multicultural and, it may be added, multieducational approach. These countries should know:

1. Which language facilitates communication among neighboring tribes, countries and the outside world
2. The extent to which interethnic communications depend on a national language
3. The impact of an official language on local structures of identity and self-esteem.

When TV is examined as a medium of instruction, many of its inherent characteristics tend to reinforce the concept of learner passivity or one way communication. Authoritative instructors are usually presented on PTV as role models and as self-contained instructional units. That concept of the learning model presupposes that learning results come from the transmission of knowledge and information in a direct line from TV set to viewer or learner.

The classroom context with an instructor and a learner may provoke a feeling of inferiority in the learner — here, the unskilled village resident. The learner may become passive toward the message he or she is being taught as a result of the inferior feeling. When this happens, the whole purpose of educating village residents through TV becomes highly questionable. Yet, some underdeveloped countries are using educational television to transmit messages to all citizens, thereby minimizing discrepancies in messages that emanate from poorly trained and/or unreliable instructors.

Effects of PTV on Lay institutions

Pedagogic TV is likely to be used improperly in rural areas unless governments provide rural areas with a two-way communication and active learning program. The decision to use TV for development education is often made on the basis of suitability. There is a certain symbolic value in establishing a national PTV schedule. PTV makes a country look modern. It leads people to believe that their government is doing something positive for them by offering formal and informal educational programs. At the same time, foreign donor countries aggressively market their technology to experimental developing countries to intimidate the latter by demonstrating their technology. PTV programs, however, are enjoyed only by those rich enough to afford a TV set. The masses do not generally enjoy that privilege. Leaders of developing countries do not seem to ask whether the price is worth the intended advantage of using the technological entity.

PTV has so far educated only a select urban audience, and the education has not helped to change the areas, going by the results of showcase projects in Samoa, Niger, El Salvador, and Cameroon. In other words, PTV has had a negative effect on the learning capacity of people in the developing world.

Any country in the Third World that assigns a high priority to rural transformation may find radio a practical medium, capable of spreading rural development messages among isolated populations that have no electricity. That approach has succeeded in several Third World countries, including Costa Rica and Nicaragua. Other studies carried out in Tanzania, Ecuador, Costa Rica, Ghana, Senegal, Guatemala, and India show that many people in the rural areas learn from radio messages. PTV may help people see what they learn, but radio is more accessible and less expensive to operate. Radio can meet the development needs of rural populations in Third World countries more than TV can.

Theoretical Framework for Analyzing Development

Development via communication has been generally classified into three operational categories: (1) the psychological approach, (2) the ideal perspective, and (3) the diffusionist approach.

The psychological approach has been amply discussed in the work of Eisenstadt (1973), who posits that the political and economic development of a society is determined by the people's psychology and their world view. The ideal approach postulates that a developing society should be able to adopt Western values in order to succeed. The proponents of that approach, Rostow (1960), Lerner (1974), and Gurevitch, Bennett, Woolacott and Curan (1982), regard development mainly from an infrastructural perspective. According to them, a society that does not turn forests into multistory buildings or build tarmac roads is primitive and underdeveloped. The diffusion approach advances that the development of an underdeveloped society depends on that society's adoption of, or dependence on, specific aid from an industrialized society. That theory presupposes that the underdeveloped society receives loans, machinery, and other hardware and software technologies from technologically advanced countries to change its environment.

This study seeks to determine whether and how development in rural communities in Africa can be supported with the simultaneous use of modern and traditional forms of communication. As such, it takes the psychological approach. In order to study rural people's perceptions about changing their systems through communication, one needs to understand and analyze the nature of transmitted messages and their effects. Since the focus of this study is on message receivers (rural people), it is important to explicate the uses receivers make of the media and then analyze the information that is diffused. An analysis of the uses and gratifications approach precedes a brief look at media effects and how diffused information can help change people's ideas or world views.

Uses and Gratifications Theory

Mass media theorists look at media behavior toward audience members in different lights. One group of theorists sees the media as having a utilitarian function; that is, media forms are useful to audiences. Other theorists perceive the media as agents of audience motivation, generating psychosocial needs in audience members who then meet the expectations of the mass media. The present study follows that concept of media-audience relationship. It posits that rural people can use both broadcast and traditional forms of communication to change and augment their lifestyles.

Uses and gratifications theory shares the assumption that a relationship exists between the mass media and the audience. Research has been done to better conceptualize the short-term and long-term effects of media influence on audience perception (Cohen, 1963; Severin and Tankard, 1979; the list continues).

The assumption that media influence lifestyles can be considered adequate in that business organizations, politicians, sycophants, attention-seekers, and governments invite media to their meetings and depend on the media to disseminate their messages. People learn about other countries and events from the mass media. However, there are controvertible views about media effects of viewers.

One such view is that media have a great influence in changing people's attitudes in a certain way. That view, upheld by the "Moderate Effect" theorists, looks at communications media as plausible channels for assessing media-audience relationships. Since the approach dwells mainly on the causal relationship between audience and mass media, it leaves researchers with questions. What kinds of processes are involved in the relationship between the mass media and the audience? What theory can adequately replicate the process of the relationship between media and audience?

In order to understand the cause-effect relationship between media and audience behavior, one has to assume that the media are the images or mirrors of a society. The concept of a society operating at the mercy of information chosen for dissemination by a few people, especially media planners, presupposes that the media are indeed capable of defining cultural boundaries and values. Littlejohn (1983) sees the mass media in terms of a society-wide, depersonalized human relationship. Tied to Littlejohn's concept is the position held by other communication scholars since Lazarsfeld that the mass media are both all-powerful and useful to the audience.

Uses and Gratifications and Media Relevance to Group Communication

The uses and gratifications approach presents a persuasive perspective to its audience. The questions that heavy TV viewers are bound to ask are:

- Do we always intentionally turn to the media for specific reasons ?

- Do all viewers have the same interests?
- What are audience members' intentions when they rely on mass media for messages?

These questions raise other questions about the credibility of uses and gratifications research and viewers' reactions in high-context cultures in developing countries. In order to understand how TV viewers in developing countries are gratified by the "moving pictures" on the TV set, it is important to describe the characteristics of media viewers.

The media-audience relationship is *per se* a communication construct that enhances interactions or discussions with mass communication scholars, students, journalists, opinion leaders, and law makers. Journalists, "educated" people, lawmakers, and politicians serve as interpreters of media messages in developing countries, since they work in media stations, own media appliances, and finance and manage the media stations.

Selectivity and interpersonal relations undermine the image of mass society as a thoughtless entity and the media as all-powerful and thoughtful (Katz and Gurevitch, 1973). Uses and gratifications theory can be better understood in light of selectivity in consuming media content. The new view of communications as selective processes was clarified by Blumler and McQuail in 1969 when they studied elections in Britain. The purpose of their study was to learn why audience members watched or avoided party broadcasts and what their choices were between watching politicians as presented on TV and voting. They hypothesized that classifying viewers in terms of motives for viewing could disclose some hitherto unrealized relationship between attitude change and campaign exposure. That study unveiled more findings about mass media effects on viewers (McLeod and Becker, 1981, p. 67).

A primary factor in the uses and gratifications approach is the view of audiences as active "prosecutors" rather than passive "consumers" of information. Viewers are seen to exhibit selective media behavior that reflects their preferences and prior interests. Media behavior is, by and large, utilitarian in that it is directed by prior motivation. However, people have the right to choose whether or not to listen to media messages. There are advantages and disadvantages in using the media of communication.

Advantages

The uses audience members make of media are laudable in that they:

- Further advance the knowledge obtained through studies of media effect
- Help the researcher to determine the extent to which such effects are related to audience members' motives and needs
- Provide a diverse look at other theories examining audience behavior that diverges from the traditional bullet or hypodermic effects and other effect studies
- Serve as a guide to possible improvements or further research techniques
- Are a means of integrating the major and minor issues of the community into medial, manageable, and procedural perspectives
- Provide adequate empirical evidence to classify statements. The Uses and Gratifications theory can contribute to the formation of public opinion and public policy in developing societies.

Kent (1928), Merriam and Gosnell (1924), and Merton (1968), in their studies of mass media and social behavior, predicted that the ultimate political effect of mass media was the retardation of social change. Due to their exhaustive research methods, their findings concerning the role of mass media in affecting social *beingness* have increased the body of knowledge available to mass communication researchers. However, innovative forms of mass media-audience research have not been exhausted. Many issues are being raised regarding the effects of the mass media on audience behavior.

The Role of Radio in Rural Development

As stated in the introduction of this study, radio is among the two broadcast media to be analyzed. The reason for selecting radio is to determine whether it would be useful to African rural people in disseminating more rural development information. Radio information can be used to sensitize rural groups to achieve most of their goals. Tusamba (1986) agrees: "L'information doit jouer un role dans le processus de revitalisation des communautés villageoises en assurant le revitalisation des masses rurales aux actions de développement" (p. 25). McAnany (1973) has identified five ways of utilizing radio for rural education and development: instruction, school, forum, open broadcasting, and animation. Among them, radio animation appears to be the most efficient medium because it encourages group participation and helps in training leaders to assist community members in defining their problems and executing development programs. Open broadcasting is also a very important strategy. Momeka (1994) concurs: "Broadcast messages are directed to an unorganized audience" and "relevant messages are capable of being accepted by the individual on his/her own" (p. 27).

Instructional radio is limited in its usefulness in that the information is directed only to a target learning group, with a supervisor directing the group and eliciting feedback. Another complication of using this strategy is that, by selecting and treating a group, the programmers give preferential treatment to certain members of a community, instead of equal treatment to all. Moreover, since rural residents operate as a homogeneous entity — which is necessary for national growth — by selecting groups and training them the authorities may be promoting factionalism. In addition, the instructional messages are often laden with ideals that contradict indigenous values. The instructors may also distort the message before it reaches rural residents.

The extent to which the instructional strategy can be used to reach a wider audience is questionable because of finance, transport and personnel considerations (Momeka, 1994, p. 29). Thus, only compact areas — small areas with a large concentration of people — can benefit from instructional radio campaigns, depending on the power of the station. Such a strategy failed in Lagos, Nigeria. Some teachers and students interviewed said that they did not listen to instructional radio broadcasts, while those who did found the broadcasts irrelevant to their needs (Dare, 1973).

The "radio schools" approach has been successful in Latin America, but with limited documentation of its use in Africa, it is difficult to determine its effectiveness in educating the rural community.

There are, however, several ways of determining the usefulness of radio for rural development, one of which is to assess its influence on rural communities in other developing countries.

Radio has been considered by communication researchers as a great agent of development. Momeka (1994) posits that radio's effectiveness depends on how it is used and for what purposes, not so much on its intrinsic qualities (p. 126). The fact that radio messages reach more people at the same time than TV messages makes radio a powerful and very influential agent of communication and change in society. Radio is even more effective than TV in changing and/or affecting the lifestyles of people in remote parts of the world. The dissemination of development programs through radio has been invariably successful, as some field researchers report.

Recent studies show the effectiveness of radio in the management of health programs. In 1988, the Federal Radio Corporation of Nigeria (FRCN) used radio and mobile vans to inform mothers about a child immunization program, the location of the clinic, and the vaccination schedule (Ogundimu, 1994, pp. 222-223). The campaign, supplemented by the Nigerian Television Authority (NTA), was so successful that a tripartite agreement was reached between the agencies and UNICEF for the latter to provide broadcasting equipment, transportation, and funding to FRCN and NTA.

Momeka (1994) also mentions cases of radio's successful performance in fostering awareness of national development plans in Senegal, Benin, Togo, and Niger (p. 134). In an earlier study conducted in Congo in the 1970s, field researcher Coldevin reported that the inhabitants heeded warnings broadcast by FAO-supported rural radio about impending contamination of their staple food crop (Coldevin, 1987, p. 89). His report is similar to many other success stories in developing countries since the 1960s.

For instance, in 1964, the first initiative to include persuasive techniques in radio programs for the education of African people was launched in Paris by the OCORA. The OCORA adapted Western radio techniques to realize techniques for the development of rural areas in Africa. The program was launched because of previous demands from such African leaders as Kwame Nkrumah, Cameroon's former President Ahmadou Ahidjo, and ministers of Information and Culture, to use radio and other forms of mass media to expedite development in their respective countries.

OCORA services and proposals for the use of "radio elements" in the form of recorded packages and written materials were first directed to French language radio broadcasting networks. The basic advantage for the receiving country was that it was allowed to redesign, edit, and change the recorded information in the imported packages to suit its local audience.

Between 1966 and 1979, the *missions de programmes* of the OCORA launched its educational plan in the Ivory Coast, followed by Mali, then Chad, Burkina Faso or Upper Volta, and then Burundi in 1979. The main objective of the *missions* was to prepare local radio stations to disseminate development information by training local production personnel and producing radio programs.

The report stated that a six-month festival was organized in the remote regions of Burkina Faso and Burundi to incite the indigenes to reflect on development, using rural radio, under the auspices of the ministers of Information and Culture in those countries. The National Rural Radio Corporation (NRRC) disseminated information to the regions competing against each other at the regional level, and finals were held at each nation's capital before its president and members of the government. Such prizes as a dispensary, an ambulance, a grange, or a herd of cattle, the report further states, were awarded to the winners.

The programs were effectively carried out in those francophone countries to mobilize and sensitize rural people. According to Coldevin (1987), a delegation of private businesspeople representing the various regions of Burkina Faso asked to join their minister in fighting usury after an energetic radio campaign launched in their village (p. 3).

In Cameroon, theme songs used to introduce rural programs may have encouraged certain villagers to listen to rural-oriented programs, because the songs are sung in indigenous languages. Also, a radio campaign was used to teach English and French to rural people. That campaign was launched in the 1970s, following the country's first referendum, to enhance national unity, education, and interaction among adult rural and urban people. The objectives for promoting national unity were fulfilled, although in some cases the campaign produced confusion among some adults. Since the adults had grown up thinking and recognizing natural forms of existence in their own ethnic languages, it became difficult to switch to a foreign language like French or English with its lexical, structural, and phonological disparities.

Nevertheless, based on the projects carried out in those Third World regions, rural radio has proven an effective agent that supports development. The effectiveness of rural radio, as noted in the cases of Burkina Faso and Burundi, is seen in the participation of rural people in entertainment programs organized by the national radio station. The campaign proves that radio messages can incite groups of rural people to become involved in team activities.

Rural Psychology and Governance

The psychology of rural individuals plays a very important part in the motivation process. Rural people tend to trust their leaders, who traditionally earned respect and power through chivalrous deeds. In most African countries, the chief, Fon, or traditional leader comes from a long line of rulers known by the indigenes to have conquered other warriors and gained territory.

Other leaders gained power through providence. This category of rulers was believed to have been "sent by the ultimate Supreme Creator" to rule the people and manage secular affairs. Such rulers, generally considered accountable only to that "Supreme Creator," have complete influence over their tribespeople, who often obey them without complaining. However, the indigenes of many African societies do not always seriously believe that their leader is intelligent, wise, infallible and strong and always decides in the best interest of his people (the leaders are usually men in most African countries). Thus rural people may effectively carry the instructions of the government media or a ruler after the latter have consulted with the indigenes. Africa's future is no longer directed by feudal princes but by modern politicians, intellectuals and, in most cases, the army. In order to understand how messages spread among such leaders and their followers, it is important to examine certain psychological obstacles to the process of communicating rural radio messages to rural people.

Some of the obstacles reported, for instance, in a study carried out by the UN Food and Agriculture Organization involve the indigenes' adherence to their steadfast values. According to the report:

> Lack of hygiene, an everyday condition, is of concern only to the medical services. Progress for women does not arouse the enthusiasm of all the male population. Nomads with nothing left in the world cannot entertain, with a tranquil heart, the idea of a sedentary life. Sacrificing the herd's oldest animal to limit the number of stock is not an easy decision. Adopting new agricultural techniques, often symbols of colonialism, presents problems (FAO Report, 1987, p.5).

Such attitudes obstruct change in the environment and decisions that may effect change. Since indigenes' attitudes constrain change or the development process, it becomes necessary to consider the use of specific forms of communication in order to determine ways of dealing with traditional taboo thoughts that obstruct necessary change. Two of those forms in Cameroon are TV and song.

Television and Traditional Media on Development Issues: Village Audience Behavior

In 1985, Cameroon television (CRTV) produced its first telecast, of Pope John Paul VI's visit to Cameroon. The national strategy for development was among other issues intended to revitalize village communities and to awaken their spirits through information programs and other infrastructures. Between 1985 and 1992, many rural residents did not have access to television because of lack of or shortages of electricity in rural areas.

Since 1985, plans for the installation of electricity have been underway in some villages and tribes, including Kom, Babanki, Nso, and other rural regions. The villagers would be responsible for the cost of their consumption. Some of the villagers do purchase TV sets, mainly to share the "magic of moving pictures" that their urban compatriots enjoy. A study of their perceptions of TV programs is justified.

Traditional Forms of Communication

While radio and television may be foreign agents of communication for people in developing countries and may pose many problems of assimilation, such indigenous media of communication as theater, song, town criers, public gatherings, and folktales have been used by the indigenes to communicate messages fairly extensively and to change their opinions and world views.

Traditional forms of communication are much older than electronic forms. Studies show that in ancient Africa, drums were used to send messages to distant lands. The sound of the drum-beat determined the kind of message intended. Messages intended to warn the clan's army against an imminent invasion were sent by way of rapid drumming, according to some elderly natives of Kom in Cameroon.

Other messages were communicated through gunshots. Gunshots in Kom and Bali tribes frequently announce the death of a community member. The sound of the gun immediately summons people to converge and mourn the deceased.

One of the better means of disseminating messages is through public gatherings of the village inhabitants. Gossip, conversation, announcements and similar word of mouth or dialogue spread rapidly when village indigenes meet at funeral ceremonies, village competitions, or market places. During market days in some villages in Cameroon, the chief, Fon, councillor, or his messengers announce future plans for the village and issues concerning the village. In Kom and Big Babanki, decisions about land disputes and other civil misdemeanors are mostly announced by the Fon and his emissaries, and they are taken seriously by the villagers.

Town Crier

Makinde (1986) has described the town crier as a communicator for rural change. Makinde (1986) suggests that the town crier serves as the mediating force for development. He writes:

> The modern town crier, as is being proposed for use in rural communication, would retain some of the trappings of his olden counterparts: He would be well-known to the community in which he operates; he would be able to speak in the language in which his audience is versed; he would understand the culture and traditions of his audience, and would possibly be a resident of the area in which he operates. He would as well imbibe the attributes of the modern communicator: fairly educated, knowledgeable of government policies, programs, objectives, and activities, and armed with government publications and a loudspeaker (Makinde, 1986).

Certainly the town crier can become a messenger for the government and the rural people and the disseminator of development information to the benefit of rural people.

Theater

Drama has proven functional and effective in communicating development information for rural masses. Traore (1972) agrees that traditional African theater has always served a social function: the education of the community. Theater conscientizes and mobilizes groups within a society (Eyoh, 1987). Theater is an effective medium for communicating messages among rural people because it is common and it creates make-believe situations that members of the community can relate to. Moreover, because Africans have a rich performing tradition through the numerous rituals, theater can become a very effective medium for conscientizing and mobilizing rural people.

In some African communities, theater has been used by educators to stimulate participation, organizational strengths of popular groups and communities, and community thinking to develop self-confidence (Kidd, 1982). The capacity of theater to depict social reality and encourage audience participation contributes to human psychological development and individual adaptation to change. According to Latin American theater analyst Boal, theater can be used to create a revolutionary consciousness within the social class structure. Human beings can use theater to achieve dignity, hope, self-expression, and self-realization in developing societies where military, tyrannic, and authoritarian regimes abound.

Institutions of higher learning have used popular theater to create a sense of awareness among mass audiences so that they can cope with government regulations. After independence, university students carried out performances in Ghana, Uganda, Kenya and Malawi to explain and promote government policies. In Kumba and Bamenda Cameroon, rural audiences worked with a cast of Yaoundé University students and university professors to produce theatrical performances that suited rural people.

The Village Herbalist

Also effective in communicating development information is the village herbalist. The villagers believe that the herbalist or "medicine man" has magical and psychic healing powers. He is familiar with and competent in treating his patients, generally the men, women, and children of the village. His medical instructions and technical advice are strongly upheld by the entire village community, including traditional administrators. A Canadian student of herbal science asserts that "herbalists and healers are trusted sources of knowledge about illness and treatment" (Riley, 1990, p. 304).

Certain governments of developing countries recognize herbalists and healers as medical practitioners and psychiatrists. In Cameroon, for instance, there exists an association of traditional doctors, which is placed under the Ministry of Health. In Ghana, a psychic's and traditional healer's association also exists. These associations collaborate with Western-trained medical personnel in treating and healing patients.

The atmosphere of cosmic power that surrounds the healer gives a patient not only more confidence in the healer but also self-motivation or the incentive to seek help. In some rural communities in Nigeria,

Mauritania, Cameroon, and Ghana, the indigenes believe that most physiological and psychological problems can be solved with cosmic powers. A Ghanaian investigator reports that indigenous Ghanaians do not believe that illness can be caused by pathological change alone. Twumasi (1975) asserts that the healer "performs acts which give the sick inspiration" and restores their own confidence (p. 35). Twumasi goes on to say that the healer

> works with the strength of his own personality and with that of the magicoreligious ritual which is part of the common faith of the society of which he is a part. In other words, the whole weight of the community, its religion, myths, history and spirit, enters into the therapy (p. 35).

The healer can act as mediator between the government and rural people. Without the participation of the traditional healer the implementation of government's health policies will be unsuccessful. Government policies may become more successful when younger traditional doctors take over from the older ones, since younger healers have a better understanding of modern health realities as community helpers.

Traditional healers can effectively convey development information to rural people and send their concerns to the government for better policy making and implementation of rural projects. All they need is instruction in more hygienic procedures from Africentric trainers to become active participants in promoting primary health care. They can stimulate a greater sense of duty and creativity among rural people. Government can use the traditional healer to disseminate its messages for the benefit of rural people, since they look to the healer for instruction. Although the villagers may find it difficult to accept foreign medicines, Western-trained doctors often spread messages in the villages about foreign ("modern") medicines and encourage the villagers to use them.

Obstacles to Communication

Certain problems prevail in traditional communication that might deter the message-sharing process, on the one hand, and obstruct its ability to reach all, on the other. The message in most traditional societies is dependent on social status. Certain people are deprived of the right to receive and use information. For instance, women in Big Babanki and Kom are not supposed to hear or share some messages disseminated by "Kwifon," the sacred messenger or medium of communication. Messages are restricted to select groups: members of secret societies and certain age-groups. Traditional leaders select message senders according to their ability to obey tribal religious principles and their attachment to the royal court. Certain messages are targeted to certain people for certain reasons.

Such obstacles in the sharing and disseminating of information to every villager lead to ignorance, suspicion, fear, mistrust, and limited interaction among villagers.

Chapter Summary

In this chapter, ways in which colonial and/or foreign cultures might have affected the interpersonal behavior of village people have been analyzed. Theories of psychophysical development were reviewed, with emphasis on the types of media that have supported and are capable of expediting rural development in some developing countries, including Cameroon.

Other issues raised in the literature include the notion that rural development does not necessarily have to entail tearing down the jungle and building houses, bridges, and tarred roads or bringing about infrastructural change. More particularly, rural development programs should contain messages that educate rural people on the necessity for self-improvement or better knowledge of health and nutrition; sensitize rural residents to creativity and more communal activity; incite open-mindedness toward taboos in tribal values and attitudes; and encourage rural residents to take advantage of available electronic and traditional media forms to augment communication and interaction among rural residents and between their village and other villages without giving up their values and their dignity.

Another issue raised is that of information sharing. An FAO report on development support communication released in Rome in 1987 asserted that the sharing of knowledge among rural populations should not involve replacing traditional communication techniques with modern ones, but merging traditional and modern systems to "produce a more appropriate hybrid, one that befits the economic and technical capacities of rural populations as well as cultural values" (FAO Report, 1987, p.

2). The immediate purpose of sharing knowledge, then, is to empower rural people to take more control over their environment and over agriculture, health, habitat, and other factors which so critically impinge on the quality of life (FAO Report, 1987, p. 2). The emphasis is on rural people sharing information among themselves in order to take control of their own environment. The destiny of Third World countries lies in their ability to develop.

In the next chapter, this study goes on to find out whether there are any communication media policies that mandate the development of rural areas and how certain governments and closed institutions use traditional forms of communication and campaigns to help change certain bad habits in the village.

A review of the literature will determine that radio and certain traditional forms of communication have been used successfully to disseminate development information for change among the rural masses. The success of the programs disseminated through radio, television, theater, village messenger or town crier, herbalist, and traditional ruler in several developing countries, including Samoa, Tanzania, Mauritania, Cameroon, and Nigeria indicates that rural people, apart from believing that electronic and traditional media can assist them in controlling their environment, may be willing to comply with government policies of change and government strategies of using electronic media to support change in their environment.

However, conclusive statements about communication effectiveness in rural development in Africa cannot be made unless African indigenes are asked for:

- Their views on whether the broadcast media have been disseminating rural development messages
- Their perceptions about their country's electronic media
- Their opinions on whether government should or should not participate in their deliberations or plans for developing their communities and their environment.

The next chapter contains a review of radio and television program logs to determine what percentage of rural development information, if any, is disseminated and how many rural people receive or consume such information. The methods to be used in answering those questions are delineated in the next chapter.

CHAPTER 5

METHODS OF RESEARCHING DEVELOPMENT INFORMATION

The Critical Approach

A dministrative or empirical researchers stress the use of quantitative techniques to generate synthesizable results, and empiricists insist that any research study must produce observable, replicable evidence. Historical/critical research offers a logistical procedure for acquiring knowledge. This approach is appropriate for research on human issues in that it demands and provides reliable information. A scientific approach is flawed in that it provides rigid answers to human issues, although human beings do not behave in a scientific way. On the other hand, the administrative approach is reliable because people's behavior change according to circumstances. Information can be acquired through hypothetical deductions or logical analyses of social issues. It involves:

1. Introducing an issue
2. Providing favorable and adverse views about the issue
3. Concluding the issue in order to provide a logical understanding.

This method entails critically and intuitively analyzing existing documents or other available data. Historico-critical research intuitively examines the role of phenomena in relation to other phenomena in order to throw more light on, or generate a better understanding, of the previous phenomena. Previous knowledge of a phenomenon under study may change based on the historico-critical arguments raised about it. The historico-critical method is mostly descriptive because it gives vivid and detailed images and simplifies understanding by providing dates and strong inferential arguments.

The use of both critical and administrative research methods in a single study should be encouraged because the combined process produces more valid and reliable results. The practice of research is, therefore, gradually advancing from monistic to pluralistic approaches. Much research in communication has not, however, used the triangulation approach, especially research pertaining to rural development issues.

The combined use of critical, content analysis, and survey methods in determining the effectiveness of communications in rural development in Cameroon is appropriate in that such methods compare the degree of correlation between messages sent to rural people by the government media and the resultant opinions formed by rural people. That triangular approach is also necessary in this study because the instruments, texts, questionnaires, and media program logs used can be reused by future investigators to retest the results generated by the present study.

Cameroon was sampled for this study because it represents Africa in many ways. It has many ethnic groups whose values are similar to those of most African societies. Most of the educated people are government employees.

The analytical process in this study had three steps: preparing data to be analyzed, coding the questionnaires, and describing them. It was necessary to use the historico-critical method to answer two of the critical questions of this study:

- What was the role of the Cameroon media in rural development?
- What was the nature of the mandate given to Cameroon media in the task of development and national integration?

These two questions have been partially answered through vivid descriptions of presidential statements in Chapter One, through historical and critical analyses of Cameroon society in Chapter Three, and the review of communication literature in Chapter Four. The answer to the third research question:

- To what extent have the Cameroon media fulfilled the terms of the mandate? requires an analysis of the content of the Cameroon mass media through examining the radio and TV program logs.

Content Analysis

Yaoundé and Bamenda radio and TV stations' program logs were analyzed to determine the number, intensity, and type of programs designed and disseminated for rural development. The government stressed national development through broadcast media messages. The Yaoundé radio and television stations usually broadcasts for the entire country. The Bamenda radio station, however, usually broadcasts in the interest of the Tikars and/or Northwestern Bantu in the Northwest province of Cameroon: the Bali, Kom, Bui, Nkambe, Momo, Bamenda and Wum areas.

The content analysis of both provincial and national radio and television programs was intended to answer the following question: To what extent have the Cameroon broadcast media fulfilled their responsibility of serving as agents of development as stated in the 1972 mandate? That question requires both policy and interpretive analyses. To determine whether the broadcast media fulfilled their responsibility of disseminating development information for rural as well as urban Cameroonians, a six-step procedure was followed when examining program logs.

1. *Distinguish rural-oriented programs from others*
2. *Count the number of times each program was broadcast per day* to determine the quantity of information broadcast and the possibility of the program reaching more people. The greater the amount of time a program was broadcast per day, the better the chance that more villagers would receive the message.
3. *Distinguish the types of rural programs from the time broadcast* to determine which one(s) the villagers were more likely to learn from.
4. *Distinguish program type, frequency of daily* occurrence, and which media broadcast the program to determine which of the media broadcast more programs;
5. *Determine the time of day the programs were broadcast* to see if the broadcast time was suitable for the village audience. Time was considered significant in that media programmers usually plan programs for specific audience segments. If more people were at home in the morning, and rural-oriented programs were broadcast then, the

messages would be more likely to raise villagers'
consciousness. By the same token, fewer people would
receive the messages if the program were broadcast when
they were not at home.

6. *Briefly describe major rural-oriented program content* in
order to determine:
• *The quantity of rural development information* (measured
by the investigator's scale of such information)
• *If the rural people would have listened or understood
the content of the program.*

Rural-oriented programs were distinguished from other programs
to determine which of them were more emphasized by the government.
Programs were classified according to language of the program and
subject or content of the program. By language was meant national or
ethnic languages. French and English are not considered indigenous
languages. The following subjects were analyzed:

- Messages on farming for rural areas
- Messages on rural health care
- Messages on rural cooperative activities
- Messages on nutrition for rural communities
- Messages on government arranged village competitions
  and,
- Messages on intervillage relations.

The number of rural-oriented programs were counted to determine
the extent to which the government emphasized rural welfare or adhered
to its principle of holistic national development. In order to determine
that emphasis, the total number of daily programs broadcast was
subtracted from that of rural-oriented programs.

Conceptual Definition of Rural Development Messages

The next step is to distinguish the types of rural programs broadcast
and the media that broadcast them, to determine

- Which rural programs contained more development
  information
- Which ones the villagers were more likely to learn from
- Which media disseminated more messages.

To understand what constituted specific messages in the program logs of the aforementioned Cameroon broadcast media (the Yaoundé and Bamenda radio and TV stations), "rural development messages" were defined in six variables: farming, rural health care, rural cooperative activities, government arranged activities in the rural community, messages on rural nutrition, and intervillage relations.

Messages on farming. These types of messages are meant to describe farmers' activities. The include testimonies from farmers about their experiences with crops, soils, and other farming methods. Some of the messages should also come from Africentric agricultural technicians on farming and/or crop production methods. Information on soil conservation techniques and related activities would also be beneficial.

Messages on rural health care. These messages discuss ways of improving the hygienic conditions and habitat of rural people. Such messages should frequently make rural residents understand what causes common illnesses like malaria, elephantiasis, typhoid fever, constipation, tetanus, and cholera and how they can be prevented.

Messages on rural cooperative activities. These messages focus on discussions about the functioning of cooperative organizations in the village community. This category also includes messages about marketing strategies and credit unions for rural businessmen and businesswomen. Testimonies from local cooperative members about their experiences with the value and process of saving money, or how to better manage "njangi" or cooperative banks and related financial agencies, would enable rural people to be more self-determined, more in control of their future, and more willing to participate in group activity.

Messages on government-arranged village activities. This category should contain information from such ministries as Information and Culture, Youth and Sports, and Town Planning, stimulating a sense of community involvement among the villagers. For instance, government may offer monthly cash prizes to villages that build the most roads and bridges, or produce the most cash crops, or keep the cleanest surroundings.

Messages on rural nutrition. Such information should be geared toward enabling rural people to eat a balanced diet. What people eat has a bearing on how long they live. Studies in several Third World countries like Nicaragua and (to a limited extent) Cameroon show that life expectancy is very short because the people have high-calorie and/or unbalanced diets.

In Cameroon, when villagers are taken ill from eating unbalanced meals, they think they have been poisoned by someone. So they turn to the herbalist for a cure. Since there are few medical facilities in the village areas, better nutrition is necessary to curb the high rate of malnutrition, death, and negligence. Messages geared toward helping rural people who watch their diet should be part of rural development.

Messages on intervillage relations. These are information tidbits that may enable each village to learn about other villages. Such messages are necessary to help reduce the high level of aggressiveness and hostility prevalent between villages. Just hearing other villagers or fellow tribesmen speak the same language used by their own people could neutralize aggressive intentions in villages and consequently unite them. Messages on intervillage relations disseminated through radio or town criers can help summon various village leaders to discuss pressing matters from their villages. That pattern of communication will not only enable their subordinates to become friendly with their neighbors but can also help in solving problems. After all, as the saying goes, two heads are better than one.

Since certain rural activities involve government officials, it is imperative that any government of developing countries understand the psychology of rural people before planning any rural-oriented programs.

Design and Method

Reliability was measured by computing the number of agreed scores obtained during coding over total scores.

The reliability (r) formula is as follows:

$$\text{Reliability (r)} = \frac{\text{\# of agreed audio-video tapes}}{\text{total of audio-video-tapes}} = \frac{13}{15} \times \frac{100}{1} = 87\%$$

More emphasis was placed on programs of the Yaoundé radio station because it was established first and is, therefore, supposed to contain more information for rural development. Programs of stations in both Yaoundé and Bamenda were sampled across at least nine years, from 1972 — when the media mandate was established — to 1994. The Bamenda station programs was sampled and analyzed from 1982 — when serious broadcasting was in effect — to 1994, while that of the nation's capital was sampled from 1972 to 1994.

Program Sampling

The sample dates for Radio Bamenda and Radio Yaoundé programs were any Monday between 1972 to 1982; any Saturday from 1983 to 1985, and any Friday from 1986 to 1994.

Among the reasons for sampling the programs between that period:

- Cameroon had its referendum in 1972. That year, the President of the United Republic of Cameroon charged the mass media with the role of disseminating development information to all Cameroonians. It is necessary to evaluate the program content of the media in order to determine if they fulfilled that responsibility.
- During the period 1982 to 1994, the new administration constantly reiterated plans for more national development. Sampling program logs according to those dates would make an assessment of the effectiveness of rural development programs more explicit.

Some program logs were analyzed using recorded audio- and video tapes owned and stored by the government in the archives of the national and provincial radio and TV stations in Yaoundé and Bamenda. Mainly programs that reflect development information covering the six variables discussed above, broadcast between 1972 and 1994, were treated to determine the type and depth of their messages.

The reasoning behind this content analysis rests on the theoretical framework advanced in Chapter Four that media audiences can make use of mass media content so long as the messages are actually sent. Measuring the degree of frequency of rural development information would determine whether Cameroon's radio and TV have been effectively fulfilling the terms of the 1972 constitution and policy statements that mandated the Cameroon media as agents of development.

Other studies of the mass media and development in Cameroon have not addressed the content of rural development information, nor have they related such content to rural people's needs. For instance, several studies are limited to development information in the Cameroon broadcast media. While they may be important to the development needs of Cameroon, they do not analyze programs containing messages on rural development specifically.

It is, therefore, important for Cameroon media planners and communication researchers to know how many programs and how much information have been available and/or sent to rural people because the rural Cameroonians make up approximately 75%, or 8.5 million, of the country's population. These population figures come from the 1989 World Bank Report.

Another reason for finding out the number of rural-oriented programs broadcast, their frequency, and the type of information they contain is the assumption that there is no effective development without an assessment of the perceptions of those who form the majority of the country's population.

The Survey Approach

The analysis of program content was supported by responses from a cross section of Cameroon rural people and government officials to determine the extent or effectiveness, if any, of communications in rural development in Cameroon. As already stated, using two or more methods (triangulation) strengthens the validity of the results accrued from a study.

To understand why the survey research method is used in this study in addition to the historico-critical and content analysis approaches to determine reliability and validity, it is necessary to provide a brief description of the survey method.

The reason for sampling in a survey is to select and discover certain norms within a population in order that a description of the norms can accurately describe standard characteristics of that population.

Since the purpose of the research was to determine people's perceptions of existing media behavior, a survey approach is necessary so that the answers given can help policymakers and/or media planners to understand how they perceive the media. Since knowledge is derived from experience, creating knowledge on existing social phenomena can improve people's socioeconomic status. Moreover, research is socially structured (Berger and Luckmann, 1966). Therefore research that involves human beings or human subjects should apply the survey method.

Sampling

The sample for this study was made up of rural Cameroonians in Kom and Big Babanki and government officials from all socioeconomic and cultural backgrounds. The richest and poorest people by Third World standards in Cameroon come from Kom and Big Babanki. Thus, they can be said to be representative of the rural and administrative populace.

External Validity

The government report VIth Five-Year Development Plan (1986, pp. 6-7), states that there are obstacles to development in the provinces including the rural areas. These obstacles include "inadequacy of collective facilities," (p. 42). The Zogid Report, compiled by the Pan African Institute for Development in 1977, also recounts similar rural development impediments in the Kombone and Mbonge rural areas in the southwest province of Cameroon. In October 1993, a government official convened a meeting of traditional municipal and political authorities to seek means of redynamizing village activities, but found that in the rural communities good drinking water and health care facilities are scarce. There are very few farm to market roads — a problem that makes transporting farm produce difficult. The external validity of rural problems in Cameroon can be established.

Although development problems in Cameroon are common to those of other rural communities in the country, the results of the interviews conducted with Kom and Big Babanki people in northwestern Cameroon are not representative of the entire rural population of Africa, since only isolated cases of common rural development problems have been recorded. Moreover, since only 126 rural people age 18 and over were interviewed, their perceptions of government media performance in rural development cannot be generalized to all rural areas of the country. The responses reflect only the views of Kom and Big Babanki people and the government officials interviewed. One can only assume that their responses would be similar to those of other rural residents in the country if the same study instruments were used.

Background of Target Audience

The Kom and Big Babanki areas have such characteristics of Third World countries as high population density, limited financial resources, and limited knowledge of health care and nutrition. Settlement in these areas is somewhat scattered. Communities are physically isolated by many hills, valleys, rivers, and insufficient roads and bridges. Situated several miles from the main urban center, the Big Babanki and Kom areas have one main route of public transport that links their areas to Bamenda for their administrative and commercial transactions. Their activities are frequently slowed down during the overly wet and dry seasons, when the road is muddy and slippery or dusty and full of potholes. On village market days, potential customers from the Bamenda urban areas are prevented by the road conditions from attending the market in rural areas. Such conditions are a devastating obstacle to the economic advancement of the villagers, who depend on such lucrative clients to buy their foodcrops and handicrafts. Moreover, with less commerce, the villagers are less capable of purchasing soap, oil, and other affordable commodities.

Kom and Big Babanki people are anxious to learn and willing to cooperate, providing the assisting entity understands their lifestyle. That esprit de corps was seen in their enthusiasm during and after interviews with the present researcher. The government subjects were also at ease with the interviewer after understanding the purpose of the study.

Specific Constituents of the Survey Study

The survey study was conducted between December 6, 1990, and December 28, 1990. This researcher consulted local quarter heads, who knew all households in the village, and asked for assistance with directions. Villages and hamlets were generally identified by separated clusters of houses, and the chief means of transport to those homes was by foot.

Three to five homes were visited per hour. Each interview lasted about 15 minutes after the preamble was translated into the local language. The Kom and Big Babanki villages were showcased for the study because the richest and poorest people (by Third World standards) in Cameroon come from there. The monthly income of both rural and government subjects was estimated from zero to 500,000 francs (CFA) and over. Husband, wife, and any male or female 18 years and above in two of every three households were interviewed because this class interacts with more people on a daily basis than the average villager. In general, one to three adults per household were interviewed.

Basically, as a descriptive project aimed at determining audience perception of government media performance in rural development, this research did not set out to determine the sample population from the entire village population. Moreover, there was no coherent document from which to determine the population size of the rural areas in question. A sample frame of the village audience could, therefore, not be estimated. So the present researcher used the village households as sample units for the males and females 18 years and over.

A systematic sampling procedure for government officials was used. The sample frame for those subjects was obtained from the civil servants' directory in Yaoundé. All government subjects in the frame must have had five to ten years of service with the government and were involved in decisionmaking in Yaoundé and Bamenda. They were chosen from among any three offices of each floor in the ministries of Information and Culture and Territorial Administration.

Two interview schedules were used to conduct the interviews, and analyses were limited to frequencies and cross tabulations.

The issues to be surveyed were:

• To what extent have the Cameroon media fulfilled the terms of the mandate given by the Cameroon government?

• How do rural Cameroonians and government officials perceive the broadcast media in the light of rural development in Cameroon?

One hundred twenty-six (126) rural subjects in 80 households and 32 hamlets were interviewed in Kom and Big Babanki. Transportation difficulties prevented the researcher from reaching more residents. The Kom and Big Babanki landscapes are hilly, and very few bridges and passable roads exist. However, the researcher visited selected farmlands and other hamlets to locate different homesteads and interview the residents there. The villagers who did not understand pidgin were interviewed in their own ethnic dialect. Respondents knew about the objectives, purpose, and significance of the study prior to the interview. They were told in a preamble not to answer any question they might consider personal and not to disclose their identity. In all, 215 human subjects participated in the interview: 89 government officials and 126 rural residents.

The survey study sought to answer a research question posed in Chapter One: How do rural people and government officials perceive the mass media in the light of rural development in Cameroon? The question sought to determine:

- If rural audience-members have had difficulty with the language of the broadcast media
- If they liked or disliked the program content of the media
- Whether they would collaborate with government officials in gathering and disseminating messages for rural development
- Whether they would prefer their own traditional media forms or the broadcast media to support development activities.

Those concerns required a "yes" or "no" response or selection of a degree of acceptance or refusal. The question also sought to know if the broadcast media fulfilled their responsibility as agents of social change. As a policy question, it sought to know if they would like both government and local media to disseminate messages for rural development.

Description of the Interview Schedule

Thirty-three questions were designed for this study to be asked of the rural and government respondents. The major questions for rural respondents sought answers to whether they owned radio and TV sets, the kinds of programs they watched or heard in those media, and what they would like the government to know regarding their attitude toward change.

The questions for government officials were meant to find out their perceptions of the country's development objectives as they pertain to the media and rural development. One of the main questions that measured the civil servants' length of service sought to know if their longevity in government posts could determine their capability in stating the appropriate policies for rural development. The question also sought to discover a civil servant's capacity to influence rural development policies within the scope of his or her ministry. A question that indexed the civil servant's place of birth attempted to determine whether time spent in the city or in the village made any difference in conceptualizing rural development policies. The interview schedules required the interviewer to fit the subject's responses into appropriate response categories in the schedule. Items in the schedule had a variety of response ranges that mostly ran from 2 ("yes" or "no") to 5, the maximum.

The questionnaire was constructed using the "Likert scale" approach. This kind of measurement, wherein a question is followed by a series of answers, helps provide more information for the researcher. Moreover, it gives the subject freedom of choice. The Likert scale method also reduces chances for vague responses, thereby facilitating the data collecting and coding processes.

Details of the statistical methods used and the analyses and interpretations of the findings from the broadcast media program logs and interviews are provided in Chapter Six.

CHAPTER 6

DATA ANALYSIS AND FINDINGS ON RADIO AND TV PROGRAMS

Content Analysis of Yaoundé and Bamenda Radio and TV Programs

Provincial and national radio and television programs from 1972 to 1994, and the responses of Cameroon government officials and rural people to these programs, were analyzed to determine the effectiveness of communications in rural development in Cameroon.

Rural-oriented programs were distinguished from other programs based on the investigator's concept of influential rural development programs. Such programs were ranked to see which of their messages had more impact on the rural people. Where necessary, codes or legends were used to indicate the meanings of words and phrases. The units analyzed were TV and radio programs broadcast on Mondays, Fridays, and Saturdays between 1972 and 1994. The unit of analysis was the program time.

Based on the thesis stated in Chapter One that development in Third World countries must be based on *Africentric* values, wherein africentric media planners and policy makers encourage rural people to engage in integrative village activities, this study focused on specific messages necessary in supporting rural development.

These specific messages were sought in the program logs of the aforementioned Cameroon broadcast media. Such "rural development messages" are defined using the six variables explained in the previous chapter.

Data Analysis of Program Content

One rural oriented radio program was purposely sampled to isolate verbs having to do with change. Verbs were considered to be capable of influencing rural listeners' views of cooperative activities, as verbs show action. Moreover, human minds tend to retain action-oriented words more than other aspects of language. Table 6 shows the amount of rural development messages in the program.

Table 6.1
Distribution of rural development messages by total number of sentences used

Program Category	Program Title	Total Program Time	Total # of Sentences	Total # of Messages
Cooperative activites	"Our Changing Rural World" (broadcast May 11, 1989)	29 min.	130	52

Percentage of rural development messages = 29

Code: 1 point scored for any verb that deals with change

Table 6.1 shows the amount of rural development messages in the program analyzed. This clearly shows the limited amount of rural development messages broadcast in that program. The argument that may be developed from looking at this is that even development programs like "Our Changing Rural World," which, by virtue of their intended audience, are supposed to contain a high percentage of rural development messages, in fact contain a relatively limited amount of such messages.

Twenty-nine percent of the entire broadcast (130 sentences) contained rural development messages. Those messages occupied 11.3 minutes of the entire broadcast time — 29 minutes. Thus, rural development messages in this so-called rural oriented program were inadequate. Although 78 phrases in the 130 sentences uttered did not contain rural development messages, they strengthened the verbs.

Analysis of Rural Development
Messages on Radio and TV

15 audio- and videotapes of radio and TV programs were purposely selected from broadcasts on Mondays, Fridays and Saturdays because normally most rural people were expected to be home to listen to radio and watch TV. Most of the programs analyzed were selected from personal collections of radio and television staff instead of from the national radio and TV archives, for the following reasons :

- Tapes recorded in 1972 were rare in the archives.
- The media stations had poor storage conditions.

The researcher depended mostly on programs recorded by some of the journalists who produced them in the 1970s.

Some of the programs broadcast after 1972 were closely compared with their titles on a program schedule compiled when the programs used to be broadcast to ensure that such titles matched the content. The chiefs of both radio stations informed the researcher that most of the radio programs were not stored on tape because of tape and space shortage. Most of the programs broadcast in those early days of Cameroon radio were destroyed shortly after use. However, certain programs had been rescheduled for several years. Thus, very few programs could be identified by year of broadcast.

Another difficulty in specifying the exact years some of the programs were broadcast was that most of the broadcasters, programmers, and chiefs of stations were replaced or fired during the period sampled, and the new officials could not find documents on programs' year of broadcast.

Using program category, time, and broadcast frequency to classify and describe the content of programs involved analyzing the program titles, time of broadcast, and program content. Rural-oriented programs were analyzed using the researcher's conceptual framework. The "miscellaneous programs" category included political party news, sports messages, music, international news, news briefs, and variety shows. The aim was to find out whether the amount of rural-oriented programing was equal to that of non rural-oriented programming. To avoid confusion in determining the content or output of the Cameroon broadcast system, one complete day's programs from one radio station was treated.

Radio station programs were measured using the ordinal interval, and ratio scales to determine the progress or status of the Cameroon broadcast media in disseminating rural development messages.

Table 6.2
Distribution of Bamenda Radio rural-oriented programs according to program time or airtime occupied per day, Time of day broadcast, and frequency of broadcast for the same Monday schedule

Rural-oriented Programs	Program Time in Minutes	Time of day Broadcast	Frequency of Broadcast
"Voices of the North West"	30	1	1
"National Languages"	55	2	1
"North-West Infos."	15	2	1
* "Provincial News"	35	1,2,3	3
"Radio Tidbits"	25	1	1

Total Amount of Program time per day = 160 minutes
Broadcast frequency per day = 7

Code:
* "Provincial News" was considered both a rural and non rural-oriented program because it contained both general information and messages about rural people's activities.
Total rural-oriented program time = 160 minutes
Total time for other programs = 495 minutes
Total amount of Monday programs per month = 655 minutes
Percentage of rural program time for Monday = 24.4 (%)
1 = Morning   5:05 a.m. to 10:05 a.m.
2 = Afternoon   11:55 a.m. to 4:59 p.m.
3 = Evening   5:00 p.m. to 12:05 a.m.

Of the 48 programs broadcast every Monday by the Bamenda station in the 1980s, only 10.4% were geared toward rural welfare. "Radio Tidbits," a program of announcements about indigenes and local administrators, spread a small amount of information for individual interest. "National Languages," a radio program wherein spokespeople from different tribes broadcast messages in their native language, could be considered beneficial to the rural people in that they did not have to struggle to articulate the psychic and ideosyncratic components of foreign languages like French and English, which Cameroon's urban residents use frequently (see Table 6.2). "Radio Tidbits," "National Languages," "Provincial News," "Voices of the North West," and "Nord-Ouest Info" could improved rapport between villagers, in that they contained information about villagers' lifestyles, activities, and projected events. However, those programs were not broadcast in the villagers' native languages.

Although the programs were broadcast within two hours of each other in each station throughout the day, perhaps to facilitate listeners' choices, they did not contain as much information on rural change as the "miscellaneous" programs, which contained non-rural development messages. Moreover, rebroadcast programs like news flashes and variety music accounted for more airtime (17 times) per day and broadcast an average of 4.5 times per day (see Table 6.3). Rural-oriented programs averaged only two hours and 35 minutes and were broadcast only six times per day.

Even the morning programs that began from 5:05 a.m. to 10.05 a.m. disseminated news and miscellaneous information eight times within approximately four hours, while only 55 minutes of airtime was allotted for rural-oriented programs. In sum, out of 19 hours and 35 minutes of programs broadcast on Mondays, only four hours and 30 minutes were devoted to rural-oriented programs. An analysis of the Bamenda rural-oriented programs shows that only 24.4% of broadcast time per Monday was devoted to such programs, while 74% was allotted for programs without rural-oriented messages. As such, the type of rural-oriented programs in the Bamenda radio station was relatively limited for its provincial listeners, to that of other programs. Moreover, three of the five rural-oriented programs were broadcast at the wrong time because 88.1% of the audience for which they were intended were away from their homes, as survey results show.

Table 6.3
Program schedule for Radio Bamenda showing program type, program time per day, time of day broadcast, and frequency of broadcast (Programs with two or more broadcast frequencies for Monday)

Program Category	Minutes and Hours	Time of Day Broadcast	# of Times Broadcast per Day
"Provincial News"	105/1.75	1,2,3	4
"The News" in French	100/1.66	1,2,3	4
"Party Activities"	210/3.50	1,2,3	5

Total amount of airtime and broadcast frequency per day = 480 minutes or 8 hours

Code:
Program time = Amount of hours or minutes in a program.
"The news in French and English" deals with National & International issues.
Party Activities is documented as "Unité—Programme Démocratie."   The program is broadcast nationally: Party members report party activities in all village and town areas of the country

1 = Morning   5:05 a.m. to 10:05 a.m.
2 = Afternoon 11:55 a.m. to 4:59 p.m.
3 = Evening   5:00 p.m. to 12:05 a.m.

To ascertain the validity of the rural subjects' response, the study measured the amount of time devoted to rural listeners of the national radio station. Since that station had more broadcast time and programs (see Table 6.4) and had been operating for several years before the Bamenda station, one would expect the national station to broadcast more development messages.

Table 6.4

Program schedule for Radio Yaoundé, the national station

Program Category	Program Time in Minutes	Time of Day Broadcast	Frequency Broadcast
General News	320	1,2,3	26
Music	120	1,2,3	6
Misc. (talk shows, general announcements, etc.)	375	1,2,3	19

Total amount of program time per day = 815 minutes
Total broadcast frequency per day = 51

Code:
1 = Morning   5:05 a.m. to 10:05 a.m.
2 = Afternoon   11:55 a.m. to 4:59 p.m.
3 = Evening   5:00 p.m. to 12:05 a.m.

The rural-oriented program, "Our Changing Rural World", formerly known as "Our Changing Agriculture", looks at development tendencies in the life of cooperative activities, agriculture, and the behavior of government agencies in the changing process of rural areas in Cameroon and in the world. "Au service de tous et de chacun" ("At the Service of -or For Each and Everyone") was also a half-hour program of news, announcements, and general information. A very small amount of messages disseminated therein pertains to rural lifestyle. However, most of the 8.5 million rural population may be likely to receive messages from these two programs, since they are broadcast nationwide.

Another program, "Islam et société'" ("Islam and Society"), was found to contain messages that could help rural people to improve their relationship with the Muslim community in Cameroon. Moreover, 16% of the country's population is Muslim (*dossier de presse,* 1983). Since some Muslims migrate, broadcasting "Islam et société" helps more Cameroonians to relate to Muslims. Such a program can improve community behavior between Muslims and other religious bodies, especially because Cameroon Muslims (Fulani) are nomadic. Communication improves mutual understanding and augments group activity. Nevertheless, message dissemination timing should be significant.

An analysis of rural-oriented program time for the Yaoundé radio station shows that out of 55 programs broadcast in 975 minutes each Friday throughout the 1980s, only 10 minutes were allotted for rural-oriented messages. The study also found that the Yaoundé and Bamenda stations had the same number of rural-oriented programs. Therefore, the national station programmers paid as little attention to rural welfare as did their provincial counterparts, and 90.9% of daily programs in both stations contained non-rural development messages.

However, rural people were more likely to receive rural development messages from the national stations from the provincial station, because more time was allotted for rural-oriented programs by the national stations (see Table 6.5).

Table 6.5
Rural-oriented programs on the national station (Yaoundé), Friday

Rural-oriented Programs	Program Time	Time of Day Broadcast	Broadcast Frequency
"Our Changing Rural World"	30	1,3	1
"Inter-Programme: Culture et Connaissance"	60	2	1
"Les Carnets du développement"	15	3	1
"Islam et Société"	25	3	1
"Au service de tous et de chacun"	30	3	1

Total amount of program per day = 160
Time & broadcast frequency = 5

Code:
1 = Morning   5:05 a.m. to 10:05 a.m.
2 = Afternoon   11:55 a.m. to 4:59 p.m.
3 = Evening   5:00 p.m. to 12:05 a.m.
Percentage of rural-oriented programs per daily broadcast = 16.4

As far as time efficiency is concerned, national station programs were broadcast at a more convenient time for village listeners than those of the provincial station. Four of the five rural-oriented programs went on the air in the evening when most of the villagers were expected to be by their radio sets at home. Broadcast time must correspond to audience listening time or audience receiving ability.

Apart from "Our Changing Rural World," relayed to the provincial stations from the Yaoundé station, all rural-oriented programs were broadcast by individual stations. An important program like "Islam et société," whose content should have been received by all rural people in the country, was broadcast simultaneously with "National Languages." The conflict might have posed program selection or listening problems for the rural listener, especially in the Bamenda area where "National languages" is broadcast. Other rural-oriented programs were broadcast at different times of day, making the reception of rural development messages difficult. Six of the 10 major rural-oriented programs — "Our Changing Rural World," "National Languages," "Au service de tous et de chacun," "Provincial News," "Islam et société," and "You and Your Health" — had a better chance of reaching the rural audience because they were broadcast in the evening (see Table 6.6). To a large extent, however, the broadcast media were less effective in disseminating rural development messages nation wide in that stations like Bamenda had a largely different rural development program schedule from the mother station. The absence of messages on nutrition on either station reflects the lack of effort by government media planners in helping rural people improve rural multi national values. Although the national station slightly edged out the provincial station in number of important rural-oriented programs broadcast, its longevity was not more beneficial to the rural people than that of the Bamenda station, since its time of broadcasting rural-oriented messages conflicted with that of the Bamenda station.

After determining that the rural-oriented programming of the station was not useful to rural people, the study further sought to prove the validity of that proposition by counting the number of times each rural-oriented program was broadcast per day over both radio stations. The counting was to determine the extent of reach and amount of message availability. The contention here is that the more times a program was broadcast per day, the greater the possibility of its content reaching more village people.

Table 6.6
Program Title, Type, Time of broadcast, and Station

Title	Program Type	Time of Day broadcast	Station
"Our Changing Rural World"	Farming	9:05a.m.	Yaoundé/ Bamenda
"You and Your Health"	Rural Health	6:30 p.m.	Bamenda
"Our Changing Rural World"	Rural Cooperative activities	6:30 a.m.	Bamenda/ Yaoundé
"Conversation"	Gov't arranged	10:30 a.m.	Yaoundé
"Rural Nutrition"	0	0	0
"Islam et société"	Inter-village relations	5:05 p.m.	Yaoundé
"Au service de tous et de chacun"	Inter-village	8:40 p.m.	Yaoundé
"Provincial News"	Inter-village	6:15 a.m.,	6:05 pm
"National Languages"	Inter-village	5:05 p.m.	Bamenda
"Voices of the North-West"	Inter-village	9:30 a.m.	Bamenda
"Folk Songs: What They Say"	Inter-village	8:30 a.m.	Bamenda

Code:
Analysis was limited to programs since 1982.
No program was found on rural nutrition.

Determining a program's dissemination time frequency required that program time for rural-oriented messages be pitted against that for non rural-oriented programs (see Figure 6.1). Results showed that the Bamenda station spent more time disseminating general news than providing rural people with rural development messages because they broadcast each program at least twice a day.

For the national station, the "Other Programs" category was split into three parts: general news, music, and miscellaneous. That station disseminated news 26 times per day, while the five rural-oriented programs were disseminated only once per day (see Table 6.7). Even music and other miscellaneous programs were broadcast 21 times per day.

It is clear that media planners paid more attention to the spreading of general public information for the population's urban minority than to disseminating rural development messages for the rural masses who make up about three quarters of the country's population.

Another task was to describe the content of major rural-oriented programs on radio. The reasons for that were:

- To enlighten the public on the content of potentially effective rural development programs
- To see if rural people might have been exposed to such content.

Figure 6.1
Distribution of daily program broadcast frequency for Yaoundé station

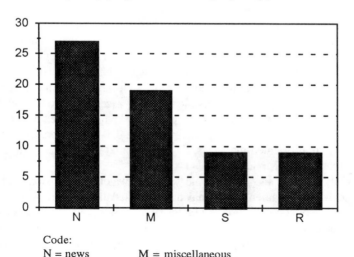

Code:
N = news   M = miscellaneous
S = musicals   R= rural-oriented messages

Table 6.7

Distribution of rural CRTV programs by broadcast time length for Friday and Saturday

Topics	Program Time in Minutes
Farming	0
Rural Health Care	0
Rural Cooperative Activities	0
Rural Government arranged Activities	0
Rural Nutrition	0
Inter-Village Relations	26

Code: 0 = no program/no message

Another major task was to find out if TV contained more rural-oriented messages than did radio. As TV has been known to raise human consciousness, and as audience members make use of TV messages, it was the present researcher's anticipation that Cameroon television (CRTV) would have more influence on the village viewers than radio. Based on the expectations of television's powerful influence on its viewers, the study traced rural-oriented messages on CRTV to determine the chances of such messages reaching rural viewers. The information content of CRTV programs was measured to ascertain whether rural-oriented messages reached the rural people. Having selected Monday, Friday, and Saturday telecasts between 1985 and 1988 as representative of heavy rural-oriented messages, the study found that no TV program was broadcast on Mondays.

Only 5.6% of the rural people surveyed watched television. The chance that rural Cameroonians may have watched the only rural-oriented program, "Nos contes favoris" ("Our Favorite Stories"), was high because it was broadcast at 7:04 p.m. TV programs were broadcast only five days per week, Wednesday through Sunday. Only 10.8% of entire TV time was allocated for one rural-oriented program. No rural-oriented programs were broadcast on Saturday. TV was, therefore, far less useful to the development needs of rural Cameroonians than was radio.

Brief Description of Media Programs

Program type: Farming
Program title: "Our Changing Rural World"
Date of Broadcast: April 14, 1989

Content Summary: "Our Changing Rural World" is a national network weekly half-hour program that discusses trends, projects, and techniques of development in Cameroon and abroad. The April 14, 1989, broadcast discussed the planting and exporting of cash crops and problems of modern agricultural extension. Its anchor person, Gudmia V. Nfonfu, discussed issues relating to the new fertilization program, including government restriction of import fertilization costs for local farmers. Guest speakers also threw more light on the subject.

Program type: Rural health care
Program title: "You and Your Health"

Content Summary: Participants on the show often advised citizens on disease prevention techniques and related health issues.

Program type: Rural cooperative activities
Program title: "Our Changing Rural World"
Date of Broadcast: May 11, 1989

Content Summary: This program provided news on credit unions. It focused on the functions of marketing organizations in Cameroon, like CAMCULD, MIDENO, UCAO, NWCA, etc. It also focused on the need to mobilize and increase credit unions in Cameroon in order to facilitate banking and loans for farmers. The program's producer, agro-journalist Gudmia V. Nfonfu, stated that "cooperative associations or apex organizations can render valuable services to primary cooperatives.

Program type: Rural government-arranged activities
Program title: "Conversation"
Date of Broadcast: October 27, 1988

Content Summary: A network program, "Conversation" examines people's ideas and activities. The guest on the October 27, 1988, show was a German production specialist who told the program's anchorman, Wain Paul Ngam, that the German government is interested in assisting Third World countries in tackling problems of development. The program provided information on the commercialization of foodstuffs in Cameroon. Dr. Guy discussed the difficulty faced by developing countries in exporting food stuffs and complained that there was a gap between Cameroon researchers and policymakers in that the researchers use sophisticated esoteric language that is not convenient for the policymakers or politicians.

Program type: Rural Nutrition
Program title: None
Program content: None

Program type: Intervillage relations
Program title: "National Languages"
Program content: None

Brief Appraisal of Rural-Oriented Radio Messages

There seems to be less emphasis by the broadcast media on making rural people aware of the importance of safer health care practices, creating and carrying out more cooperative activities, and encouraging more intervillage relations. Messages intended to support rural farming and/or agricultural activities were disseminated more frequently compared to other development entities, and the percentage of farming messages was heavy.

One major way of disseminating rural development messages is through agro-pastoral trade shows. The Cameroon government has been organizing national agro-pastoral shows once every two years in major cities of the country. The show that allegedly started in Buea in 1973 brings together hardworking, skilled farmers and craftspeople. These people compete with farmers from other villages, and prizes are awarded by the government for the best products. The main purpose of the show is to enhance development in the town hosting it.

Several cases of bribery and corruption between some government officials and rural crop producers have been reported. The Produce Marketing Organization (PMO), which to a certain extent used to cater to the production and marketing needs of local farmers, recently laid off hundreds of its workers, leaving farmers with limited resources and choices. The produce marketing board should be demolished to give the farmer direct access to the world market, but the farmer's immediate income and profit depend heavily on that farmer's knowledge of better production techniques.

During 1972 and 1994, when rural-oriented programs were traced and measured, very few rural residents were invited by the radio program producers to articulate their perceptions of disseminating development messages through communication channels in their villages. Since rural people best know their social milieu, they should be given a forum to express their own concepts of rural change. They have the full right to state how communication can support change in their community. Partially based on the latter argument, this study surveyed the opinions of Cameroon rural people and government officials. The analyses and findings of the survey are discussed in Part II of this chapter.

Survey Research Findings: Data Interpretation

Survey Anatomy

A survey study of Cameroon rural people and government officials was carried out. No significant audience perception research had heretofore been done regarding the effectiveness of communications in rural development in Cameroon. Also, no known study has been carried out to determine the opinions of both rural people and government officials in the Ministries of Information and Culture and Territorial Administration regarding the use and/or effectiveness of the broadcast and traditional media for the dissemination of rural development messages.

Major studies regarding the mass media in Cameroon have mainly suggested what the Cameroon policymaker should do to promote development in Cameroon with the support of the mass broadcast media. More audience surveys are needed, especially of the Cameroon masses, rural people, to determine their perceptions of rural change because they constitute the country's majority population. Such studies should find out whether more rural development messages may have been broadcast since Cameroon's referendum.

In the present study, rural people were asked questions about their perceptions of the broadcast system, and the perceptions were compared with those of government officials in two ministries related to rural welfare, to determine whether the broadcast media were effective in spreading messages on rural change. Responses on traditional modes of communication from Kom and Babanki village people were also examined to see if such modes could be more effective than radio and TV in expediting rural development in Cameroon.

Results

Of the one hundred twenty-six (126) subjects surveyed, 41 or 32.5% owned radio and TV sets, while 11.9% did not own any broadcast media equipment. Eleven (11) subjects did not answer the question (see Table 6.8).

Table 6.8
Owners of radio and TV

Value Label	No. of Subjects	Percentage
Radio	52	41.3
TV	7	5.6
Both	41	32.5
Not interested in any	15	11.9
Abstentions	11	8.7
Total	126	100

Asked why they owned such equipment, 52.4% of the 100 rural subjects who answered the question said they received news from radio and TV (see Table 6.9). The present investigator went on to find out whether Cameroon radio and TV made the viewers aware of Cameroon issues. 66.7% of the rural subjects strongly believed that those media made them aware, as compared to 0.8% that did not believe so.

Table 6.9
Reasons for using radio or TV set

Value Label	No. of subjects	Percentage
To get news	66	52.4
To get sports and Entertainment Information	21	16.7
To boost my ego and financial ability	11	8.7
To know about the government	2	1.6

The study inquired the extent to which most of the rural radio and TV owners depended on these media by asking them whether they would like specific programs disseminated by those media. The specific programs included "Our Changing Agriculture", "Our Changing Rural World," and health instructions. Of the 125 rural subjects who answered the question, 38 or 30.2% strongly supported the concept that radio and TV frequently disseminated such programs. Eighty-eight percent (88.1%) of them generally agreed that the broadcast media should disseminate rural-oriented messages, while only 3.2% were strongly opposed to the idea.

Given subjects' overwhelming need to have more rural development messages in the broadcast media, this researcher went on to investigate what language they would like the programs broadcast in. The reason for measuring language against program was to find out whether the rural people had been or might be bothered by the use of foreign languages on Cameroon radio and TV for the dissemination of messages in their interest.

Since more than 75% of Cameroon's population comprises village people, this researcher's speculation was that rural people would prefer their own local languages to English and French, frequently used on radio and TV. 31.7% of the rural people upheld the present researcher's position, 27% preferred to receive in English and French, and 1.6% did not consider the use of any specific language an issue.

Having determined the subjects' enthusiasm in seeking general messages from those media, the researcher went back to Question Number II which sought answers to the villagers' source of messages about village matters, since many of them (31.7%) wanted messages from radio/TV disseminated in their own indigenous language.

After finding that rural people got most of their information about village issues from community gatherings, the researcher scaled the local modes of communications to determine:

- Which of those forms the villagers used the most
- Whether they preferred using specific local forms of communication or radio and TV to disseminate rural development messages
- The feasibility of using local forms for disseminating rural development messages in rural Cameroon.

The rural subjects said they got most of their information from community gatherings (see Table 6.10).

Table 6.10
How villagers get most of their information about their village

Value label	No. of subjects	Percentage
Radio	31	24.6
TV	5	4.0
Both	42	33.3
Community gatherings	48	38.1
Other	0	0
Total	126	100

A cumulative percentage of 99.2 rural subjects used local forms, as opposed to 79.4% radio and TV audience. Table 6.11 shows that town criers were the most preferred medium, followed by word of mouth with 31%. The third most used medium was the theater, with 19.8% responses.

Asked why they preferred local media to broadcast media, 65.1% of rural subjects said that local media were part of their culture and that they grew up using local media to interact with their peers. Thirty-one percent said they did not understand French and English spoken on the radio and TV, so they used local media; 3.2% preferred local media because they could not afford a radio or TV set.

Table 6.11
Frequency layout on the use of local media

Value label	No. of subjects	Percentage
Theaters	25	19.8
Town criers	42	33.3
Gong/ nguh	4	3.2
Market	14	11.1
Word of mouth/hearsay	39	31.0
Songs	1	0.8
Other	1	0.8
Total	126	100

The study proceeded to find out when village people were at home to listen to rural-oriented messages on radio or TV. The reasons for doing that were twofold:

- To know whether the rural audience had missed much rural-oriented information on radio and TV by using local forms of communication and, therefore,
- Whether the broadcast media really fulfilled their responsibility as agents of social change in disseminating rural development messages during times that were convenient to the rural audience.

The analyzed Yaoundé and Bamenda radio and TV programs proved that most of the rural-oriented messages were broadcast in the afternoon. The survey revealed that 88.1% of rural subjects were in the fields, markets, and elsewhere when most of the rural-oriented messages were sent; 11.1% of the rural subjects were not at home in the morning, nor were 0.8% in the evening.

Since village Africans generally carry out their activities according to the weather conditions, it was inappropriate for media programmers and policymakers to schedule most rural-oriented programs during daylight, when village people normally take advantage of tropical sunlight to perform outdoor chores. Thus, the times for rural-oriented broadcasts were inconsistent with their audience's interest and listening ability (see Table 6.13).

Given that media messages are meant for specific audiences, this study has, to some extent, proven that the Cameroon mass broadcast media did not effectively fulfill their responsibility as agents of social change as far as the rural people are concerned. Messages intended to support rural development were sent at a time when rural people were not around their radio or TV sets. Moreover, many rural people indicated that they were not getting most of their messages from radio and TV. In addition, relatively few and insufficient rural-oriented programs were broadcast on TV and radio, as opposed to non rural-oriented programs.

Table 6.12
Purpose for using local media

Value label	No. of subjects	Percentage
Grew up using them	82	65.1
Don't understand the language on radio/TV	39	31.0
Have no money to buy radio/TV	4	3.2
Have no time to listen to radio/TV	1	0.8
Total	126	100

Table 6.13
Distribution of rural people's daily chore schedule

Value label	No. of subjects	Percentage
Morning	14	11.1
Afternoon	111	88.1
Evening	1	0.8
Total	126	100

The next step was to find out whether government officials in decision making positions were aware of the insufficiency of rural-oriented programs in the mass media. First, the study compared rural people's responses regarding broadcast media performance with those of government officials to know whether rural people's perceptions of the Cameroon broadcast system were legitimate. The latent rationale for cross-examination was to get an accurate account of the effectiveness of communications in expediting rural development in Cameroon.

The first question asked of government officials was "Would you say that so far, the government is doing well in developing the rural areas?" to ascertain their perceptions of the country's development objectives and to determine whether the government had been pursuing its principle of balanced development in the rural areas as vigorously as in the urban areas. The stated degree of success was measured against the subject's years of service, based on the assumption that the more time a government official spent in a government position, the better the official's chances of conceptualizing and stating appropriate policies for rural development.

A civil servant's capacity to make meaningful statements concerning rural development information was also based on the amount of time the official spent in the village community. Amount of time spent in the village could make a difference in the articulation of rural problems and the conceptualization of rural development policies.

The results from Question 1 show that 71.9% of the government subjects felt the government was not doing well in developing rural areas, while only 4.5% thought the government was doing well; 12.4% thought that the government was doing a mediocre job in developing the rural areas, and 7.9% refused to answer the question (See Table 6.14).

Table 6.14
Would you say that so far government is doing well in developing rural areas?

Value label	No. of subjects	Percentage
yes	4	4.5
no	64	71.9
Probably yes	11	12.4
I don't know	2	2.2
No response	8	9.0
Total	89	100

The study went on to distinguish subjects' views concerning government performance in rural development by the amount of time spent by the respondent in that government position. Of the subjects who had spent 16 or more years in any decisionmaking position, 21.9% believed that the government had not been doing an effective job of developing the rural areas. Nearly thirty-three percent (32.8%) of those who had served the country for six or more years held the same opinion. Thus, the more time a government official spent in a decisionmaking position, the greater the official's awareness of government's poor performance or limited degree of commitment to rural development.

How long did they live in the village before becoming civil servants? The question sought to learn whether more time spent in the village enabled the civil servants to understand rural people's information needs and whether that understanding might have any impact in their ability to conceptualize development policies.

Of the subjects who answered that question, 87.5% upheld the view that government had not been doing an effective job in developing rural areas. Thus, the researcher's assumption that government was not doing enough to develop the village areas was upheld.

Who were those government officials, anyway? They were top officials in the Ministries of Information and Culture and Regional Planning/Territorial Administration. Researchers accounted for 11.2% of those surveyed, directors 14.6%, secretaries general 2.2% (who by

Cameroon standards are ranked next to ministers), and 60.7% were journalists, chief secretaries, wardens or heads of penitentiary personnel, assistant heads of bureaus, chiefs of service, and deputy directors.

Although 60.7% of the subjects held influential government positions, up to 28% of the more influential decisionmakers — directors, researchers, and secretaries general — who felt that the Cameroon government had not done an effective job developing rural areas. This demanded a deeper investigation. Did all the civil servant subjects have the same opinion of the broadcast media's performance in gathering and spreading rural development messages? The investigation was also intended to learn of any difference in the previous perception of government attitude toward rural development.

The government subjects were asked to state their opinions of how government should support rural-oriented programs. Journalists, wardens, secretaries, assistant heads of service, and deputy directors indicated the need for government to design and execute rural-oriented programs. Over sixty-two percent (62.3%) of them stated that government should:

- Use the media to educate rural masses on the dangers of poor health and nutritional practices
- Send teams to the rural areas to hold seminars and workshops with rural people about their living conditions
- Encourage the use of more local media.

Only 3.3% of the secretaries general and 9.8% of the directors agreed to all three suggestions. Twelve and a half percent (12.5%) of the subjects refused to answer the question. Because only 12.5% answered the question, one can say that influential decisionmakers in Cameroon tend to be reluctant to share certain information about the government. Even the government researchers, who are supposed to be objective in handling social issues, including rural welfare, were somewhat skeptical on the idea of sending teams to rural areas and/or encouraging the use of local media in disseminating rural development messages. Only 13.1% of them approved of all three proposed government activities.

The study further pursued the responses of rural subjects to see if there was a significant difference between their perception of the role of the Cameroon media in supporting rural development in Cameroon and that of government officials. Subjects were asked to answer the following question on a scale of one to five: Should programs such as "Our

Changing Agriculture" and health instructions be broadcast frequently on radio and TV?   A total of 88.1% favored the use of such programs containing relatively heavy amounts of rural-oriented messages.

A certain class of government officials, journalists, deputy directors, etc., in that category (62.3%) shared the same perception held by rural people that the Cameroon mass media should broadcast specific programs with heavy quantities of rural development messages.

The study then went on to investigate their attitudes toward government participation in rural people's activities. Rural subjects were asked to state their opinions on a scale of one to five as to whether they wanted radio and TV personnel to attend village gatherings and report their proceedings to other villages. The main objective of the question was to see whether village people had any reservations about government's participation in their private matters.

To share information is to share power. Information-sharing increases understanding, and more understanding, increases interaction and participation. Using radio and TV to spread ideas on village issues can increase community involvement. Hence, particular radio and TV messages can support change in the rural community. Out of 126 rural subjects who were asked to state the extent to which they would like radio and TV crew to audit and report on their meetings, 82.5% generally agreed that it would be appropriate, while 17.5% did not want a government crew to join them. Of those who agreed, 27% were somewhat skeptical of the benefits of admitting any government crew, while 52.4% felt comfortable with their answer. Only 3.2% of the subjects said they would strongly welcome the idea of allowing radio and TV personnel in their meetings.

After receiving the consensus response from most rural subjects and from 62.3% of government officials that more programs should be disseminated by the Cameroon broadcast system, the researcher decided to compare the demographics of the respondents to see whether sex, age, and income made any difference in attitudes toward the Cameroon broadcast and traditional media. The primary reasons for measuring sex against age, for instance, were:

- To find out if responses about the effectiveness of communications might have been affected by financial situation, chronological age, or sex
- To know whether a subject's gender was a factor in that subject's world view of communications.

Out of the 126 subjects, 88 were male and 36 female. Of the male subjects, 86.2% had a monthly income of between 15,000 francs CFA and 40,000 francs CFA. None of the rural subjects earned more than 151,000 francs, CFA. There was no evidence that sex or income affected responses. Female subjects' responses were then compared to males about the use of sacred local media (flutes, drums) to see if the data suggested that females responded out of loyalty to males. Another purpose for the comparison was to determine whether such female loyalty (if any) would become a factor if traditional media were used in disseminating messages for rural change.

The major local media selected by the rural subjects were as follows: town criers 33.3%, word of mouth 31%, and theaters 19.8%. Results showed that 85.7% of the 42 respondents who used town criers were male and 14.3% female. Of the 39 respondents who used word of mouth, 64.1% were male, 35.9% female. Sixty percent of the 25 subjects who used theater were male and 36% female. Female subjects favored the use of local communication forms for the dissemination of rural development messages as well as the male subjects. Since more than half of the male and female subjects answered the question, females did not seem to be actually yielding to the rural males on these topics. Moreover, 50% of both female and male subjects said they used the gong/"nguh," which happens to be operated by the clan's male only.

Did age play any role in the subjects' attitude toward the effectiveness of communications in rural development? The rationale for considering age against responses was to find out which of the age groups answered more questions about using communication to support rural development. Results show that 48.4% of young people between 26 and 30 years of age expressed their feelings toward rural welfare by providing useful information that could help Cameroon media planners and developers in programming and executing rural development. More than fourteen percent (14.3%) of rural subjects aged 18 to 25 years held similar positive opinions about using rural-oriented messages to help change the rural environment. On the whole, more young people answered the questions that demanded rural change through communication than did older people; only 0.8% of rural subjects aged 51 years and over participated in the interview. That percentage difference indicates that young people were more likely to discuss issues concerning rural change than older people (see Table 6.15).

Table 6.15
Distribution of Age and Rural Audience Responses

Age of rural respondents	No. of subjects	Percentage
18-25 years	18	14.3
26-30 years	61	48.4
31-50 years	45	35.7
51 years and up	2	1.6
Total	126	100

Conclusion

This study set out to determine the effectiveness of communications in rural development in Cameroon by way of analyzing broadcast and traditional mass media in Cameroon.   Two rural communities were showcased: Kom and Babanki (Kijem). The study looked at "effectiveness" in terms of the quantity and quality of rural-oriented messages in the Cameroon broadcast media, the amount and quality of messages sent to rural audience members, and the extent to which the messages reached them. Message quality was determined by the number of verbs dealing with rural change in any rural-oriented program broadcast. The effectiveness of communications was further determined by the messages sent to the rural people and their receiving time and by the responses given by the audience members concerning the quality and amount of those messages in the Cameroon broadcast media.

The message-sent criterion was determined by carrying out qualitative and quantitative analyses of national (Yaoundé) and provincial (Bamenda) radio and TV program logs to determine the amount of rural-oriented messages.

The study compared rural-oriented programs with other programs between 1972 and 1994. The quality of rural-oriented messages was determined by selecting verbs that indicated change. Six conceptual categories of rural development messages (see Chapter Five) served as the researcher's framework for analyzing the content of 1972-1994 radio and TV programs in Cameroon.

Effectiveness was determined by finding out what types of programs were broadcast, the period when the programs were broadcast, the number of times such messages were broadcast, and whether the target audience, rural people, could have been at home by their radios and TV sets to receive such messages.

The data showed that people preferred using such traditional communication modes as theaters, town criers, markets, and face-to-face interactions for the transmission of messages, rather than radio and TV. traditional media were seen as potentially effective media for the dissemination of rural development messages.

The study also provided brief socioeconomico-historical analyses of Cameroon's administrative and political structures. The historico-critical method partially discussed the mandate assigned to the Cameroon media by the government as agents of development. A triangulation approach was used in the study to determine whether communications in Cameroon were effective in supporting rural development between 1972 and 1994.

To fortify the arguments of whether the mass media broadcast enough development messages, a content analysis of program logs and survey methods was used. As rural people make up over 75% of the entire Cameroon population, the study sought to know whether there was effective communication between rural people and government officials.

The study found that:

1. The Cameroon mass media have been largely focusing on entertainment. Even news broadcasts have been dealing with international issues rather than with domestic issues.
2. There were not enough rural development messages broadcast by the Yaoundé (national) and Bamenda (provincial) stations. A very limited number of programs broadcast by those stations contained rural development messages. Since most of the programs were broadcast in French and English, languages not understood by many villagers, very little of the rural-oriented messages was really useful or meaningful to the rural people.
3. Most rural-oriented messages did not reach their target audience because they were broadcast in the afternoon, while the villagers were away from their homes.

4.   Few rural people had radio and TV sets. Messages sent
     through those channels could not be quickly and effectively
     shared by the rural people. Also, the risk of distorting
     such messages could have been great since only a few
     received them first hand. Misinterpretations usually lead
     to misinformation and low output.

5.   Both rural people and, surprisingly, government officials
     agreed that the Cameroon government had not done well
     in developing rural areas or disseminating enough rural-
     oriented messages.

6.   Many rural people and government officials felt that
     government did not support rural development.

7.   The villagers favored traditional modes of communication
     over radio and TV because they were accustomed to using
     local modes of communication. The local modes were
     found to be potentially more effective in disseminating
     messages than were radio and television. Local
     communication modes would, therefore, be more effective
     than radio and TV in spreading messages that support rural
     development.

Generally, the Cameroon broadcast media did not effectively
disseminate enough rural development messages for Cameroon rural
residents. The cumulative quantity of messages intended for the rural
people was hardly more than 25%. The messages were sent at the wrong
time and did not always reach their audience.

Thus, there is a need for procedures that would enable effective
dissemination of rural-oriented messages and/or support of rural
development in Cameroon. Suggestions and recommendations for a
new development communication agenda for Cameroon and other
African communities appear in the final chapter of this study.

CHAPTER 7

FINDING A NEW COMMUNICATION AGENDA FOR RURAL DEVELOPMENT

A frican governments have suffered many setbacks in the process of development. In Cameroon, for instance, the following problems still deter that process:

- The capability is limited to assess constructive programs necessary for expediting massive development among its citizens, and governments have not normally allowed free information dissemination in African countries.
- Mass media continue to disseminate more messages in support of government and non-development-oriented issues like sports, music, and other entertainment, regardless of whether such messages serve the larger community for which the government is established.
- Large segments of the population remain helpless in the face of problems and obstacles to development.

The major consequence of the government's control of mass media content is that development is held back. The mass media operate for the masses and, therefore, the masses should have the right to set media agenda. In Cameroon, where the government preaches democracy and democratization to its citizens, it should demonstrate the doctrine by allowing the people to choose their media programs and messages. In reality, policies regarding the mass media and other institutions are determined by the government.

Since generations of Africans have lived under colonial administration, and imbibed colonial cultural taboos, development efforts in Africa will be heavily influenced by foreign concepts. For instance, as described in Chapter Three, Cameroon has many cultures, both indigenous and foreign. It will be difficult to merge those cultures and to integrate Cameroonians. Since members of the over 256 ethnic groups speak different languages, changing ethnic world views would be difficult. However, as suggested in the literature review in Chapter Four, communication can support development efforts, no matter what people's philosophical orientations.

The broadcast and traditional mass media can support rural development programs and promote Africentric concepts of change by carrying out mass campaigns in the rural areas and raising rural consciousness about such issues as proper health care, nutrition, respect for community -oriented activities, and better intervillage relations. Such a media campaign would increase villagers' self-awareness, further integrate the rural people, and promote a spirit of communality or collective activity.

Africa will scarcely develop if their governments do not use the values of the masses to set their development agendas. Indigenous values should be influential factors in the formulation of national laws and policies. Laws relating to freedom of expression are best developed when the governments, in close collaboration with local rulers, fit the indigenes' ways of life into national development agendas. A government cannot authenticate and put into action its principles of integration and national unity until it meets regularly with village leaders, synthesizes their major values, and bases its legislation on those values.

Media dissemination of tribal values would enable the masses that make up about 80% of Africa's population to understand and support government principles. Indigenous translators and interpreters can be trained to translate the concerns of both government and rural people on TV or radio into the languages the masses understand well. Foreign administration agendas are inappropriate in Africa since the majority of Africans think in terms of their own language and culture. An appropriate model for the formulation of social and administrative policies is necessary not only to ensure not only a more meaningful function for the African mass media, but also to develop collective objectives for uniting the people and developing the country (see Figure 7.1).

Figure 7.1
Model for implementing social and administrative policies in Africa.

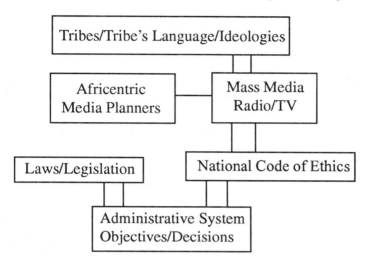

Legend: The single and double lines linking the rectangles show the importance of the connection in the making of social and administrative policies in Cameroon

Between 1972 and 1994, the Cameroon mass media failed to live up to the mandate determined by the heads of state and reiterated by the ministers of Information and Culture. They did not disseminate enough qualitative and quantitative information to support rural development. The following steps should be taken to expedite rural development in Cameroon.

More rural oriented programs that contain messages on rural health-care, nutrition, cooperative and government-arranged activities, inter-village relations, and farming methods are needed on radio and TV to sensitize and motivate rural people toward effective development. Any rural development initiatives should involve the rural people.

Setting the Broadcast Media Agenda

Scheduling

Since rural-oriented programs tend to be broadcast at times when most rural people are unable to receive the messages, the Ministries of Information and Culture should develop a strong research institute with Africentric mass communication technicians to conduct periodic surveys of rural people's daily schedule in order to determine the appropriate times for broadcasting rural-oriented messages.

Radio and TV Programming

The use of village idioms to spread development messages would increase villagers' consciousness of concepts that optimize local resources and minimize tardiness. Messages in local languages spread quickly via radio since radio reaches many rural people. Showcase countries include Costa Rica, Kenya, Tanzania, and several Third World countries. However, since most villagers cannot afford a radio or TV set, village leaders and village-trained campaign teams should organize sessions once or twice a week wherein radio and TV listeners meet and report or dramatize the rural development messages they hear for those who cannot afford such appliances.

Media planners need to increase program content and schedule about seven or eight rural-oriented programs per day. Prior to determining the types of messages to be increased, program planners should consult with village leaders and media agenda-setters should use Africentric concepts of development when selecting messages for rural audiences, since most Africans observe African values (see Figure 7.2). They should look at messages that can motivate rural residents to think for themselves and to do what is comfortable for them. Programs should reflect ancestral values and project ways in which such values can be used to tackle contemporary problems in the rural areas.

Reflecting on the ancestral values to be included in the media agenda begins with the training of media personnel.

Figure 7.2
Proper climate for effective communication to support rural development in Africa

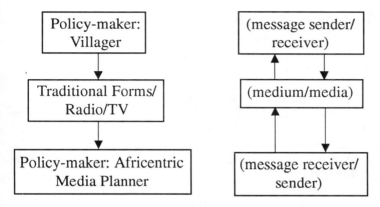

Legend: The media appear in order of preference.

Training Personnel

Since the majority of Africa's population is rural, research should be largely based on improving rural lifestyle. The government staff assigned to work with rural people should have prior experience with the indigenous psyche of the rural people. Researchers and technicians should first become participant observers. They should become familiar with the anthropological and historical lifestyles of the people before carrying out any field study. Third World audience-oriented research has not closely examined at the problems of method, theory, and pragmatics or the cultural paradigms of the indigenes.

Deconstructing Foreign Languages

Most rural people in Africa do not usually want to listen to messages disseminated in English, Portuguese, French, or any foreign language. Rural people in Cameroon need the input of media agenda-setters to:

- Make "National Languages," usually broadcast by the Bamenda station, a network program that villagers of all 256 "ethnic" groups in the country can receive rural oriented messages first-hand in their own language.
- Employ more indigenous translators and broadcasters who understand French, English, and at least seven indigenous languages, in order to translate and broadcast rural development messages in the indigenous language.

If these were done, rural residents would get more rural development messages with less strain. They would be more interested in (listening to) rural-oriented programs when they heard their own language spoken on such programs.

French and English should not be taught because they are both psychologically and economically costly for rural residents. In psychological terms, European languages can suppress the villagers' language, thinking procedures, and the values that underlie them and promote the very Eurocentric attitude that has been chiefly responsible for many African countries' underdevelopment. Teaching English and French to villagers would cost the government (which does not have a balanced economy) a good deal of money, because instruction in English and French would have to begin from the grassroots and it would take many years to teach over 8.5 million-and-growing rural citizens two foreign languages.

Communication During Agro-Pastoral Expositions

Agro-pastoral expositions in Cameroon usually take place every two years. The shows are set up to appraise the production of agricultural and related products with implications for the infrastructure development of the host town and neighboring areas. Government should punctuate the activities of the agro-pastoral show with radio messages about rural development. Such messages should also be disseminated through graphic literature: pictures of a healthy village lifestyle and illustrations of, for example, how people drink standing water and get sick or die. Other radio messages should include TV or live dramatizations of better farming methods and lucrative cooperative activities. The messages should express better ways by which the villagers can form credit unions/ "njangi" and save their proceeds. Such messages should be occasionally blended with traditional music and live comedy from the village area.

There seems to be great willingness among rural residents of Cameroon to cooperate in any government or collectively determined endeavor, as long as they get the right help.

As indicated in their responses to most of the questions in the survey, these people are prepared to improve their way of life, if provided with rural-oriented messages by the government and media. In order to enhance media campaigns, the government should ask village leaders to assemble dynamic youth in the village and ask them to spread information throughout the neighborhood on good health care, better intervillage relations, and better agricultural methods.

Using Traditional Media

Such traditional media forms as live theaters, town criers, marketplace and word of mouth are popular among African rural people in terms of their longevity of use and their effectiveness in transmitting messages. In the past, these forms were used to disseminate folklore and general information among the people. Local media has proved useful to them; things got done and society flourished. Traditional media forms can be used efficiently to disseminate rural development messages among the village people.

Town Criers

Town criers, in many rural areas, are village messengers who go from one village to another delivering messages from the village authorities. In some tribes these messengers walk the village streets spreading news from the village headquarters. Occasionally striking a gong, they report the news to the attentive village audience. A typical message in Tikari villages in Cameroon is usually delivered as follows:

> Every one should listen (silence in households). Fon (ruler of the kingdom) has asked me to greet you. He has said that every man and woman should appear at the village market area before sunrise.

Then he goes on to state the purpose of the meeting. He usually gives only the news headlines, thereby arousing the villagers' interest. This strategy of suspense gets most people to attend the meeting. The purpose of the meeting often ranges from publicly tackling crimes or misdemeanors to announcing plans for constructing major roads and bridges or helping a resident build his homestead. This medium is also used to warn the people of impending epidemic diseases.

Since the kingdom's ruler has influence over the villagers in Kom and Babanki, he could become an effective communicator of more rural development messages in those communities. Moreover, like the town crier, he is well known in the village because he speaks the language they understand.

The Marketplace

Studies by Odoku (1987), Awa (1988, p. 3), and other scholars in development communication see the market as an effective medium of communication. Many ideas and messages are exchanged in the market by people from different areas. Awa (1988) reports that the African market has been used successfully by "pseudo-pharmacists" to sell non prescription and sometimes prescription medicine to hundreds of people attracted by loudspeakers (p. 137). Messages on the values of better nutrition and inter-village relationships, for instance, can be spread by local people trained by Africentric technicians (see Figure 7.2).

Masked Dancers (Masquerades)

Masquerades, or what is known in African English as "juju," are respected by villagers, who believe that such entities have supernatural powers. Some of them are, however, masked human beings. Those beings can deliver rural development messages directly from the Foin or the village head, to the rural residents.

Word of Mouth

A communication paradigm used by many rural people, as seen from the survey results of this study, is word of mouth, which can become the most efficient medium for transmitting rural development messages. All it takes is an influential villager to start a rumor, say, about someone who died from constantly eating food left out overnight. Such a rumor would spread very fast, for the village is a close community, and every bit of information is shared as soon as it becomes available. Good and bad news spread through rumor faster than through other channels of traditional communication.

Social Gatherings

Apart from market places, such places as bars, private homes, the Fon's palace, funerals, weddings, and farmlands can become outlets for spreading rural development messages. Many people attend events whose masters of ceremony are either herbalists or family members, such persons should be advised by the Fon or household head to motivate the people to exploit their talents and skills. The leaders should tell the people to use their skills in produce useful products they can market and to preserve their ancestral wisdom.

Live Shows and Fairs

Village authorities should organize more frequent expositions where skilled villagers an exhibit their products. There would be better output in villages if events were organized about six times a year where villagers could display, receive prices for, or sell their best products. Prizes should also be awarded for information-sharing skills between exhibitors. Such shows should rotate among the villages, so that other villagers can gain experience.

Monitored Communication

Finally, certainly not least, there should be a monitored communication channel between government or law makers and villagers to facilitate the flow of rural development ideas and messages (see Figure 7.2). Above all, better media policies for rural development should be made and implemented early to prevent rural people from depending heavily on government, since certain government policies are predicated upon values suitable only to members of Western and Eastern societies.

In order to maintain and/or strengthen that channel, or make communication more effective in the development of rural communities in Cameroon, rural development policies should always involve village representatives like the village head. The villagers should always be allowed to decide the types of messages to be spread or the means of receiving them, since they best understand their needs. Although radio and TV are capable of transmitting much rural development information, traditional modes of communication should be used more vigorously because they are cheaper, more accessible, more portable, and more familiar to rural people in African countries.

References

Africa South of the Sahara (1994). 23rd edition. London: Europa Publications. p. 120.

Ahidjo, A. (1968). *The Political Thought of Ahmadou Ahidjo*. Monaco: France.

Ainslie, R. (1966). *The Press in Africa: Communication, Past and Present*. London: Victor Gollancz.

Akpey, C. R. N. (1978). *The Effect of Denominational Education on Social Relationships among the Kom People in Cameroon*. Cameroon: Afo-a-Kom Publications.

Ambekar, J.B. (1992). *Communication and Rural Development: A Village in North Karnataka*. New Delhi, India: Mittal Publications.

Ardener, E. (1956). *Coastal Bantu of the Cameroons*. London: International African Institute.

Asante, M. K. (1987). *The Afrocentric Idea*. Philadelphia: Temple University Press.

Awa, N. (1988, Fall). Communication in Africa: Implications for development and planning. *Howard Journal of Communication, 1* (3), 131-143.

Ayittey, G. (1992). *Africa Betrayed*. New York: St. Martin's Press.

Ball, P., Palmer, P., & Millward, E. (1986). TV and its educational impact: A reconsideration. In J. Bryant, & D. Zillman (Eds.), *Perspectives on Media Effects*. Hillsdale, NJ: Lawrence Erlbaum Associates.

Bandolo, H. (1985). *La flamme et la fumée*. Yaoundé, Cameroon: Éditions SOPECAM.

Bayart, J. F. (1980). One-party government and political development in Cameroon. In N. Kofele-Kale (Ed.), *An African Experiment in Nation Building: The Bilingual Cameroon Republic Since Reunification* (pp. 159-187). Boulder, CO: Westview Press.

Beltran, L. (1976). TV etchings on the mind of Latin Americans: Conservatism, materialism, and conformism. *Gazette, 24* (1).

Berger, P. & Luckman, T. (1966). *The Social Construction of Reality: A Treatise on the Sociology of knowledge* . Garden City, NY: Doubleday and Co.

Berrigan, F. (1977). *A Manual on Mass Media in Population and Development*. Paris: UNESCO.

_____ . (1981). *Community Communications: The Role of Community Media in Development*. No. 90. Paris: UNESCO.

Biya, P. (1987). *Communal Liberalism*. London: Macmillan.

Blake, C. (1993). La fin des visions eurocentriques. *Développement: Revue de la société internationale pour le développement*. pp. 8-11.

Boafo, S.T. (1987). Africa must rethink its course in communication. Media Development: *Journal of the World Association for Christian Communication, 34*, 14-16.

Bois, J. (1968). *Communication as Creative Experience*. Los Angeles, CA: Viewpoints Institute.

Bologh, R. (1979). *Dialectical Phenomenology: Marx's Method*. Boston: Routledge & Kegan Paul.

Caldwell, J. (1969). *African Rural-Urban Migration: The Movement to Ghana's Towns*. Canberra: Australian National University Press.

Carruthers, J. & Karenga, M. (1986). *Kemet and the African Worldview*. Los Angeles, California: University of Sankore Press.

Chaffee, S. & Hochheimer, J. (1985). The beginnings of political communication research in the US: Origins of the limited effects model. In M. Gurevitch and M. Levy (Eds.), *Mass Communication Review Yearbook V* (pp. 75-104). Beverly Hills, CA: Sage Publications.

Chilver, E. M. (1966). *Zintgraff's Explorations in Bamenda, Adamawa, & the Benue Islands: 1889-1892*. West Cameroon: Ministry of Primary Education & Welfare.

Church, G. (October 18, 1993). Anatomy of a disaster in Somalia. In *Time* Magazine (of USA), 142 (16), 40-48.

Cohen, B. (1963). *The Press and Foreign Policy*. Princeton, NJ: Princeton University Press.

Coldevin, G. (1987). *Perspectives on Communication for Rural Development: Food and Agriculture Organization* (FAO) Report. Rome, Italy: Development Communication Branch, Information Division.

Costeodat, R. (1930). *Le mandat français et la réorganization des territoires du cameroun* (pp. 118-119). Besançon, France: Jacques et Demontrond.

Dahrendorf, R. (1959). *Class and Class Conflict in Industrial Society*. Stanford, CA: Stanford University Press.

Dare, O., et al. (1973). *Consumption of Schools Broadcast in Secondary Schools in Lagos*. Sessional project essay. Lagos, Nigeria: Department of Mass Communication, University of Lagos.

Devereux, S. (1993). Observers are worried: Learning about the language and counting people in northeast Ghana. In S. Devereux and J. Hoddinott (Eds.), *Fieldwork in Developing Countries*. Boulder, Colorado: Lynne Rienner Publications.

Dodds, T. (1972). *Multi-Media Approach to Rural Education: Case Studies*. International Extension College, Broadsheet on Distance Learning, No. 1, London.

Dossier de presse. (1983). Ministry of Information and Culture. Yaoundé, Cameroon: MINFOC Publication.

Edeani, D. (1990). The Nigerian press in a depressed economy. In N. Ikechukwu E. (Ed.), *Mass Communication and National Development*. Aba, Nigeria: Frontier Publishers.

Ejedepang-Koge, S. (1985). *Change in Cameroon*. Alexandria, VA: ARC Publications.

Eisenstadt, S. (1973). *Tradition, Change, and Modernity*. New York: John Wiley & Son.

Eyoh, N. (1987). Theatre and community education : The African experience. *Africa Media Review, 1* (3).

Faringer, G. (1991). *Press Freedom in Africa*. New York: Praeger Publishers.

Ferretti, F. (1975). *Afo-a-Kom: Sacred Art of Cameroon*. New York: The Third Press.

Fishman, J. A., Ferguson, C. A., & Jyotirinda, D. G. (Eds.) (1968). *Language Problems for Developing Nations*. New York: John Wiley.

Food and Agriculture Organization Report. (1987) Rome, Italy: Development Communication Branch, Information Division.

Forje, C. W. (1981). *The One and Indivisible Cameroon: Political Integration and Socio-Economic Development in a Fragmented Society*. Lund, Sweden: University of Lund, Department of Politics.

Fuglesang, A. (1978). *Applied Communication in Developing Countries: Ideas and Observations*. Uppsala, Finland: The Das Hammarskjold Foundation.

Greenholm, L. (1975). *Radio Study Group Campaigns in the United Republic of Tanzania*. Paris: UNESCO.

Guiffard, A. (1989). *UNESCO and the Media*. White Plains, NY: Longman.

Gurevitch, M., Bennett, T., Woolacott, J. (Eds.). (1982). *Culture, Society and the Media*. London: Methuen and Company.

Hall, E. (1977). *Beyond Culture*. Garden City, NY: Anchor Books.

____. (1980). Cultural studies and the centre: Some problematics and problems. In S. Hall, D. Hobson & A. Lowe, & P. Willis (Eds.), *Culture, Media, and Language* (pp. 15-47). London: Hutchinson.

Herbert, T. (1981). *Dimensions of Organizational Behavior*. New York: Macmillan.

Hoffman, M. (1993). *The World Almanac and Book of Facts 1993*. New York: Pharos Books.

Katz, E., Blumler, J. & Gurevitch, M. (1973). Uses and gratifications research. *Public Opinion Quarterly, 3*, 510-521.

Kaunda, K. (1994). President Kaunda's speech in *The Hilltop* (of Howard University, Washington, DC) 77: A2.

Kent, F. (1928). *Political Behavior*. New York: Morrow.

Kenyatta, J. (1968). President Kenyatta airs ownership question. *I.P.I. Report*. July/August.

Kidd, R. (1982). Plays for farmers: Popular drama workshops in Northern Nigeria. *Theatre International, 6* (2), 27-40.

Kofele-Kale, N. (1981).*Tribesmen and Patriots: Political Culture in a Poly-ethnic African State*. Washington, DC: The University Press of America.

Kulakow, A. (1984, May). *A Definition of Development Communications*. (manuscript). Washington, DC: Academy for Educational Development.

Lamb, D. (1986). *The Africans: Encounters from the Sudan to the Cape*. London: Methuen.

Langer, J. (1979). *Theories of Development*. New York: Holt, Rinehart, and Winston.

Lazarsfeld, P., Berelson, B., & Gaudet, H. (1948). *The Peoples' Choice*. New York: Columbia University Press.

Lerner, D. (1958). *The Passing of Traditional Society: Modernizing the Middle East*. New York: The Free Press.

_____. (1974). Mass communication and the nation state. In W. P. Davison, & F. T. C. Yu (Eds.), *Mass Communication*. New York: Harper & Row.

Le Vine, V. (1964). *The Cameroons: From Mandate to Independence*. Los Angeles, CA: University of California Press.

Lipmann, W. (1922). *Public Opinion*. New York: Macmillan.

Littlejohn, W. S. (1983). *Theories of Human Communication* (2nd ed.). Belmont, CA: Wadsworth Publications Company.

Luostarinen, H. (1991, October). Innovations of moral policy in the Gulf War. In M. Traber & P. Lee (Eds.), *Media development* (pp. 10-14). London: Battley Brothers Ltd.

Mattelart, A. (1976). *Multinational Corporations and the Control of Culture*. Brighton, England: Harvester Press.

Macbride, S. (1983). *Final Report of the International Commission for the Study of Communication Problems*. (p. 448). Paris: UNESCO.

Makinde, K. (July 8,1986). A modern use for the town crier. *The Standard* (of Nigeria).

Malek, A. & Leidig, L. (1991, October). US press coverage of the Gulf War. In M. Traber & P. Lee (Eds.), *Media Development* (p. 15-20). London: Battley Brothers Ltd.

Matip, M. (1985). Cultural identity and the mass media. *The Cultural Identity of Cameroon*. Yaoundé: Ministry of Information and Culture.

McAnany, E. (1973). *Radio's Role in Development: Five Strategies of Use*. Washington, DC: Information Center on Instructional Technology.

McLeod, J. & Becker, L. (1981). The uses and gratifications approach. In D. Nimmo & K. Sanders (Eds.), *Handbook of Political Communication* (pp. 67-95). Beverly Hills, CA: Sage Publications.

McLuhan, M. (1964). *Understanding Media: The Extensions of Man*. New York: McGraw-Hill.

McQuail, D. (1983). *Mass Communication Theory: An Introduction*. London: Sage Publications.

Merriam, C. E. & Gosnell, H. L. (1924). *Non-Voting*. Chicago: Chicago University Press.

Merton, R. K. (1968). *Social Theory and Social Structure*. New York: Free Press.

Meryowitz, J. (1985). *No Sense of Place: The Impact of Electronic Media on Social Behavior*. Oxford: Oxford University Press.

Ministry of Finance. (August, 1986). *VIth Five-Year Economic, Social and Cultural Development Plan ,1986-1991*. Yaoundé, Cameroon: MINFIN.

Ministry of Information and Culture. (1983). *Dossier de presse*. Yaoundé, Cameroon: MINFOC Publications.

_____. (1985). *Cameroon News*. Washington, DC: Embassy of Cameroon.

_____. (1986). *Cameroon in Brief.* Yaoundé, Cameroon: MINFOC Publications.

_____. (1986). *Cameroon in Brief.* Yaoundé, Cameroon. MINFOC Publications.

_____. (1988). History of Cameroon. In *National Yearbook*. Yaoundé, Cameroon: MINFOC Publications.

Ministry of Planning and Territorial Administration. (1985). Yaoundé, Cameroon: MINPAT Publications.

Momeka, A. (1980). *Reporters Handbook*. Lagos, Nigeria: Department of Mass Communication Press.

_____. (1994). Radio strategies for community development: A critical analysis. In Andrew A. Momeka (Ed.), *Communicating for Development: A New Pan-Disciplinary Perspective*. New York: State University of New York press.

Monroe, B. (May, 1991). How to cover War: Forget the Pool. In *Washington Journalism Review*.

Mowlana, H. (1986). *Global Information and World Communication: New Frontiers in International Relations*. New York: Longman.

_____, Gerbner, G., & Schiller, H. (Eds.) (1992). *Triumph of the Images: The Media's War in the Persian Gulf-A Global Perspective*. Boulder, CO: Westview Press.

_____. (1993a, Summer). Toward a NWICO for the twenty-first century? In *Journal of International Affairs*, *47*, 1, 59-72.

_____. (1993b) Communication and Development: Everyone's problem. In *Interactions*, *xi*, 1, 3-25.

Nelson, H., et al. (1974). *Area Handbook for the United Republic of Cameroon*. Washington, DC: Department of the Army.

Nfonfu, V. G. (1989). Producer, "Our Changing Rural World." National Radio Network Station, Yaoundé, Cameroon.

Ngam, P. W. (1988). Producer, "Conversation." National Radio Network Station, Yaoundé, Cameroon.

Ngwainmbi, E. K. (1992). *Dawn in Rage*. Calcutta, India: Writers Workshop.

Ngwa, J. A. (1978). *A New Geography of Cameroon*. London: Longman.

Nkrumah, K. (1964). The role of the revolutionary press in Africa. *African Mirror 8*, 8-10.

Nkwi, P. N. (1976). *Traditional Government and Social Change: A Study of the Political Institutions among the Kom of the Cameroon Grassfields*. Fribourg, Switzerland: University of Fribourg Press.

Nooter, H. M. (1993) *Secrecy: African Art that Conceals and Reveals*. New York: Museum of African Art.

Nwabuzor, E. (1980). Ethnic value distance in Cameroon. In J. N. Paden (Ed.), *Values, Identities, and National Integration*. Evanston, IL: Northwestern University Press.

Nwanko, R., & M'Bayo, R. (1989). The political culture of mass communication research and the role of African communication researchers. *Africa Media Review 3* (2), 9-12.

Odoku, J. (1987) From indigenous communication to modern television: A reflection of political development in Nigeria. *Africa Media Review 1* (3), p. 3.

Ogundimu, F. (1994). Communicating knowledge of immunization for development: A case study from Nigeria. In Andrew A. Momeka (Ed.), *Communicating for Development: A New Pan-Disciplinary Perspective*. New York: State University of New York Press.

Pan African Institute for Development (1977). *Village Profiles* (Zogid Profiles No. 2 RES/ZOG/SER.E/3/77) Du Sautoy College, Buea, West Cameroon.

Pool, I. (1961). The mass media and politics in the modernization process. In L. E. Pye (Ed.), *Communication and Political Development* . Princeton, NJ: Princeton University Press.

Preston, W., Herman, E., & Schiller H. (1989). *Hope and Folly: The United States and UNESCO 1945-1985*. Minneapolis, MN: University of Minnesota Press.

Program of Advanced Studies in Institution Building and Technical Assistance Methodology (1976, June) (p. 4). Indiana University.

Revue de L'Urtna: Développement des systèmes radiodifussions (1981). Dakar, Sénégal.

Righter, R. (1978). *Whose News? Politics, the Press and the Third World*. London: Burnett Books.

Riley, M. (1990). Indigenous resources in Africa: Unexplored communication potential. In *Howard Journal of Communication, 2* (3), 301-314.

_____. (1993). Indigenous resources in a Ghanaian town: Potential for health education. In *Howard Journal of Communication 4* (3) 249-264.

Rodney, W. (1982). *How Europe Underdeveloped Africa*. Washington, DC: Howard University Press.

Rogers, E. M. (1976). *Communication and Development: Critical Perspectives*. Newbury Park: CA: Sage Publications.

_____. (1978). The passing of the dominant paradigm: Reflections on diffusion of innovation research. In W. Schramm & Daniel Lerner (Eds.), *Communication and Change: The Last Ten Years and the Next*. Honolulu, HI: The University of Hawaii Press.

_____. (1989). An Inquiry in development communications. In M. K. Asante & W. Gudykunst (Eds.), *Handbook of International and Intercultural Communication*. Beverly Hills, CA: Sage Publications.

Rostow, W. W. (1960). *The Stages of Economic Growth*. Cambridge: Cambridge University Press.

Rubin, R. B. & Perse, E. (1989, February). Attribution in social and para-social relationships. In *Communication Research, 16* (1), 55-77.

Sarti, I. (1981). Communication and cultural dependence: A misconception. In E.G. McAnany & J. Noreon (Eds.), *Communication and Mass Media Research*. New York: Praeger Special Studies.

Schiller, H. (1969). *Mass Communications and American Empire*. New York: Augustus.

_____. (1976). *Communication and Cultural Domination*. New York: International Arts and Sciences Press.

Schramm, W. (1964). *Mass Media and National Development*. Stanford, CA: Stanford University Press.

_____, W. (Summer, 1983). The unique perspective of communication: A retrospective view. *Journal of Communication 33* (3), 6-17.

_____, & Lerner, D. (Eds.). (1978). *Communication and Change: The Last Ten Years and the Next*. Honolulu, HI: University of Hawaii Press.

_____, W., Siebert, F., & Peterson, T. (1956). *Four Theories of the Press*. Urbana, IL: University of Illinois Press.

Sengat-Kuo, F. (1984). Speeches on Cameroon National Radio Station.

Severin, W. & Tankard, J. (1979). *Communication Theories: Origins, Methods, and Uses*. New York: Hastings and House.

Speagle, R. E. (1972). *Educational Reform and Instructional Television in El Salvador: Costs, Benefits, and Payoffs*. Washington, DC: Academy for Educational Development.

The Herald (of Cameroon). 1993-94.

The New Fon of Kedjom Keku (Big Babanki) in the Grassfields of Cameroon (1983). Basel, Switzerland: Prescraft.

Thomas, S. Phiri, O. , Mbuein, D., Laiser, M., & Mpetsane, Z. (18th February-10th March, 1972). *Zone Study Report: Fundong Sub-Division, Mentchoum Division*. Buea, Cameroon: Pan African Institute for Development.

Todaro, M. (1976). *Internal Migration in Developing Countries*. Geneva: UN Fund for Population Activities.

Tsurutani, T. (1973). *The Politics of National Development: Political Leadership in Transitional Society*. New York: Chandler Publications.

Traore, B. (1972). *The Black African Theatre and Its Social Functions*. Ibadan, Nigeria: Ibadan University Press.

Twumasi, A. (1975). *Medical Systems in Ghana: A Study in Medical Sociology* (p. 35). Accra, Ghana: Ghana Publication Corporation.

Tusamba, R. (November, 1986). Radio cameroun et développement rural. In *Le magazine du monde rural*. Genève: Institut Universitaire d'Études du développement.

Ugboajah, F. (1985). *Mass Communication, Culture and Society in West Africa*. New York: Hans Zell Publishers.

Verba, S. (1965). Communication and political culture. In Lucien Pye & Sidney Verba (Eds.), *Political Culture and Political Communication*. Princeton, NJ: Princeton University Press.

Vogel, S. & Ebong, I. (Eds.). (1991). *Africa Explored: Twentieth Century African Art*. Prestel, Munich: Center for African Art.

Wagao, H. J. Tanzania: The impact of adjustment. In Giovani, C., Hoeven, R., & Mkandawire, T. (Eds.) (1992). *Africa's Recovery in the 1990s: From Stagnation to Adjustment to Human Development*. New York: St. Martin's Press.

Wells, A. (1972). *Picture-Tube Imperialism: The Impact of US Television on Latin America*. Maryknoll, NY: Orbis Books.

Williams, P. (1991). Let's face it, this was the best war coverage we've ever had. *Washington Post 17*, 3.

Index